Let

the Living Waters

Flow

By Jan Coverstone

Jan Coverstone

Let the Living Waters Flow

By Jan Coverstone

Published by JC Life Books Columbia City, Indiana USA
by Createspace
ISBN: 978-1-72224-599-3

Religion / Christian Life / Spiritual Growth

www.jancoverstone.com

Discover other books by Jan Coverstone

Spiritual Warfare: Understanding Biblical Truth & Satan's Deceptions
The Spiritual Truth Series:
Vol.1 The Gifts, Grace, and Flow of the Holy Spirit
Vol 3 How You Think Determines Who You Are

In memory of Paul E. Paino whose teachings

still reverberate through my mind and life.

Jan Coverstone

Acknowledgements

I thank the Lord Jesus Christ, the Holy Spirit, and our Heavenly Father for giving me the opportunity to learn and grow in my understanding of the gift and ministry of prophecy. It has enriched my life, so much so that I cannot imagine serving the Lord without using this gift.

I also thank the church family (ecclesia: the called out ones) of Christian Fellowship Church who believed in what I was being led to explore, and not only supported the work, but personally became involved and practiced what was taught. Without their love and encouragement, this writing would not have happened. It is an honor to serve such a willing group of saints, and I thank them from my heart and all that is in me.

I want to include a special thanks to Matt and Naomi Ritter for their love and support, and also for typing the original manuscript. May you be blessed richly for your faithfulness!

To Rocky and Amanda Burns: Eternity alone will reveal your rewards for your love, encouragement, and prophecies, which strengthened my spirit and helped more than these words could ever express. As Aaron and Hur held the arms of Moses, the two of you have held me in your arms and held my arms so that I could progress. Thank you.

I wish to thank Ron Hults for his friendship, support, and encouragement.

To all who read this material, I thank you for allowing this book to be a part of your life and journey. May the eyes of your understanding be opened, and may your spirit be always willing to manifest the love of our Father, the Lord Jesus Christ, and the Holy Spirit into the lives of others by your spoken words.

Jan Coverstone

Foreword

I have had the honor of knowing Pastor Jan Coverstone for nearly thirty years, and in that time, I have known him to be a conscientious and caring man of God. As a pastor, he places the oversight of his flock on his daily list of priorities. He also places a high priority on the word of God.

Jan ministers from the Bible, carefully supplementing for accuracy and practicality. He is concerned that followers make a personal application of God's word in their daily lives. Pastor Jan has systematically studied the word of God and thoroughly reviewed the various workings of the Holy Spirit with special attention to the gifts. He believes the Lord speaks today as clearly as he did to the prophets and apostles through the gift of prophecy.

Being bi-vocational for most of his pastoral ministry, Jan Coverstone has demonstrated being a Christ follower in both working environs. Specifically, he proactively seeks to communicate through the prophetic gift of God's love and his desire to relationally connect with everyone.

Let the Living Waters Flow is Jan's graphic endeavor to communicate his and Christian Fellowship Church's exceptional experience with living a prophetic lifestyle. The New Testament declares that prophecy in the church age is to edify, exhort, and comfort, and that the spirit of prophecy is the testimony of Jesus.

You will discover when you read this book this local church is successfully exercising prophecy to minister to people sharing love that transcends all of life.

Dennis Kutzner has served CMI GLOBAL as a pastor to pastors and church consultants for over thirty years and now heads Global Church Connection, which is committed to growing healthy churches. He is also an associate consultant with Church Doctor Ministries, specializing in risk assessment.

Table of Contents

What is Prophecy?

Prophesy: a verb, propheteuo, to speak by divine inspiration. (Strongs Concordance, 4395)

Prophecy: a noun, propheteia, the speaking forth of the mind and counsel of God; the declaration of that which cannot be known by natural means. (Vines Expository Dictionary of New Testament Words)

God speaks to his people through his word, the Bible. He speaks to us in many ways, but he has chosen to work and speak through faithful believers by the gift of prophecy. To prophesy is to speak inspired words under the blessing of the Holy Spirit to edify, exhort, and comfort. In my understanding, this is to be sensitive to the guidance of the Holy Spirit and to be willing to share what the Spirit leads you to say to bring blessing and healing to those you are speaking to. The prophetic words flow from God's heart and are a spoken manifestation of his love.

*And above all things have fervent charity among yourselves: for charity shall cover the multitude of sins. Use hospitality one to another without grudging. As every man hath received the gift, even so minister the same one to another, as good stewards of the manifold grace of God. If any man speak, let him speak as the oracles of God; if any man minister, let him do it as of the ability which God giveth: that God in all things may be glorified through Jesus Christ, to whom be praise and dominion for ever and ever. Amen. (*1 Peter 4:8–11)

Follow after charity, and desire spiritual gifts, but rather that ye may prophesy. For he that speaketh in an unknown tongue speaketh not unto men, but unto God: for no man understandeth him; howbeit in the spirit he speaketh mysteries. But he that prophesieth speaketh unto men to edifcation, and exhortation, and comfort. He that speaketh in an unknown tongue edifieth himself; but he that prophesieth ediifeth the church. I would that ye all spake with tongues, but rather that ye prophesied: for greater is he that prophesieth than he that speaketh with tongues, except he interpret, that the church may receive edifying. (1 Corinthians 14:1–5)

Jan Coverstone

Part I

The Power of Words

If you have not taken a vow of silence, then words are a part of your daily life. For some, communicating may be the greatest aspect of your life. Do we stop and think about the words that we are using? We know the Word of God has power, but have we considered the power of our words? Proverbs 18 and verse 21 tells us "Death and life are in the power of the tongue, And those who love it will eats its fruit."

Do we bring blessing into our lives by our words, or do our words bring strife and stress into our lives? That is a choice we make or allow when we speak. This first section looks at the power of our words through biblical examples to explore the possibility of our words affecting our lives more than we realize.

Chapter 1

And God Said

Then God said: "Let there be light" and there was light. (Genesis 1:3)

I have marveled at the depth and complexity of this simple verse, *"let there be light."* It is straightforward and to the point. The word was spoken, and it was done. The earth revolves around the sun every year. The earth is tilted at the perfect angle, resulting in the change of seasons. It was started with one command. The light was divided from darkness.

"Then God said, "Let there be a firmament in the midst of the waters, and let it divide the waters from the waters…And God called the firmament Heaven. So the evening and the morning were the second day." (Genesis 1:6, 8)

This "firmament" was a great canopy of water vapor that covered the earth, diffusing the sun's rays to uniformly heat the planet. The great oil and coal deposits are clear evidence of that firmament, because they prove that the earth was once covered with lush vegetation over most of the planet.

God spoke the world and all of his creations into existence—all of the animals, fish, birds, and man. It was all started by speaking. Verses 9, 11, 14, 20, 24, and 26 all begin with *"Then God said."* We cannot fathom the power of God's words. We can read the account of creation and accept it but to understand the depth of multiplied trillions of molecules forming in such diverse ways is way beyond our finite mind. However, since God is that powerful and almighty to create such a wonderful, magnificent universe, he also is more than able to help us with our (rather small by comparison) struggles and perplexities in our daily lives. He may speak one word to us and change our lives.

Isaiah 50 begins with the Lord speaking and asking rhetorical questions. *"Is my hand shortened at all that it cannot redeem? Or have I no power to deliver?"* (Isaiah 50:2)

No, his hand is not shortened and he can still reach into our lives. He spoke, and a world was framed. His words carry the weight of ultimate authority. His word is ultimate truth.

The apostle John started his gospel with these words: *In the beginning was the word and the word was with God, and the word was God. He was in the beginning with God. All things were made through him and without him nothing was made that were made. In him was life, and the life was the light of men.* (John 1:1–4)

"*And the word became flesh and dwelt among us, and we beheld his glory, the glory as of the only begotten of the Father, full of grace and truth.*" (John 1:14)

We know this is written of Jesus Christ who, as the second member of the Trinity, was the manifold and manifest word of God before taking on the form of man. His words have power:

Then he arose and rebuked the wind and said to the sea, "Peace, be still," and the wind ceased and there was a great calm, but he said to them; "Why are you so fearful? How is it that you have no faith?" And they feared exceedingly and said to one another; "Who can this be that even the wind and the sea obey him!" (Mark 4:39–41)

In Mark 5, Jesus spoke to a man with unclean spirits that, upon hearing his word, obeyed and left the man. He was clothed, whole, and in his right mind. Later, Jesus healed a woman who touched his clothes by saying (confirming her faith), "*Daughter, your faith has made you well. Go in peace and be healed of your affliction.*" (Mark 5:24–34) His words have power.

In the same chapter, verse 41, "*Then he took the child by the hand and said to her; "Talitha cumi,'"* which translates to "Little girl, I say to you, arise." His words restored the child to life. His words have power.

Jesus said, "*It is the spirit who gives life, the flesh profits nothing. The words that I speak to you are spirit and they are life.*" (John 6:63)

The words of the Lord are *pneuma*, and they are *zoe*. They are from the Holy Spirit, and they contain and give life. His words, spoken some two thousand years ago, are as relevant for us today as when he first spoke to his disciples. They are eternal. They have power. They have life.

Luke tells of Jesus sending out seventy disciples to talk about the kingdom of God. When Jesus sent the seventy out. He gave them authority. He ordained that their words would have power. His commission to his disciples gave them authority, and the outpouring and infilling of the Holy Spirit to the believers in the upper room on the day of Pentecost gave them power. Peter stood and preached, and three thousand souls were born of the Spirit in response to the word, and they were added to the church, the body of Christ.

They returned with joy, saying, *"Lord even the demons are subject to us in your name."* (Luke 10:17) They had power behind their words when they spoke as his servants doing his will. The physical and the spirit realms were both subject to their words when they were acting under orders from the captain of their salvation. The disciples prayed for and anointed the sick and the sick were healed.

The gospel of Matthew closes with this: *All authority has been given to Me in Heaven and on earth. Go therefore and make disciples of all nations, baptizing them in the name of the Father, and of the Son, and of the Holy Spirit, teaching them to observe all things that I have commanded you; and lo, I am with you always, even to the end of the age.* (Matthew 28:18–20)

And he said to them: "Go into the entire world and preach the gospel to every creature. He who believes and is baptized will be saved; but he who does not believe will be condemned. And these signs will follow those who believe. In My name they will cast out demons, they will speak with new tongues, they will take up serpents, and if they drink anything deadly it will by no means hurt them; they will lay hands on the sick and they will recover." So then, after the Lord had spoken to them He was received up into Heaven and sat down at the right hand of God. And they went out and preached everywhere, the Lord working with them and confirming the word through the accompanying signs. (Mark 16:15–20)

Christ told his disciples *"But you shall receive power when the Holy Spirit has come upon you; and you shall be witnesses to me in*

Jerusalem, and in all Judea and Samaria, and to the end of the earth."
(Acts 1:8)

When Christ told his disciples that his words were spirit and life, they heard and believed him. The power of his words hasn't changed to this day. We have the Holy Spirit, and he brings the words of Christ to life in our lives. We share life with others by our words. But, for most of us, our words do not always breathe life into those around us.

"Death and life are in the power of the tongue, and those who love it will eat its fruit." (Proverbs 18:21)

Our words can bring destruction and death into the lives of others, if they flow from a heart that is not fully surrendered to the Author of Life and Prince of Peace. If our words are harmful to others, our words will bring that same spoiled fruit into our own lives. If we speak good, life-giving words to others, we will have that fruit (result) of our words reflected in our lives too.

The act of blessing is the transferring of benevolence, praise, or encouragement by the spoken word. When Isaac blessed Jacob, that younger twin brother lived out his life under the positive spiritual influence and power of his father's blessing, even though the father had intended it for Esau. When Jacob (whom God renamed Israel, "Prince of God") blessed his sons and Joseph's sons, what he said came to pass. What he spoke over them became reality in their lives. Do we bless and give life to others or are too many of our words harmful and destructive?

Do we understand and believe in the power of our words? We know the Bible shows us the power of God's word, but do we honestly know and believe our words have power? Our words insinuate either life and blessing or pain and destruction into our lives and in the lives of those whom we influence.

Have you seen a child's face responding to the sting and force of harsh words spoken to him? Have you felt the impact of bitter, cutting words? We can each probably answer yes to both questions.

Have you watched a child's reaction when something good was said to them? How about yourself? How blessed and uplifted you are by good, life-giving words spoken to you? We delight in being encouraged and uplifted and know the crushing pain we suffer when we are torn by hurtful and malicious words. Words have power.

I believe what the word of God teaches about words. I preached almost every Sunday for one year on the power of words. This series of sermons was life-changing—both for people in the congregation and for myself. Words are the most used and misused power tools we have in our daily interactions. This book is written to explore and manifest how we may use our words to change our lives and the lives of those with whom we speak.

Te best testimony is personal experience. Ron, our home church worship leader, had this story to share. One night, the Spirit impressed upon him to be very careful about his words for the next three days because the things he'd say would come to pass in very clear ways. Good or bad, what he said was going to happen. He was very careful, actually a little fearful, not wanting anything bad to happen to anyone as a result of his thoughtless utterances. He also did not want to offend God by trying to win the lottery or by saying something out of his carnal desires and not according to the will of God. Everything went well until one night. He tied up his Doberman Pinscher, Zeke. He was a good size by Doberman standards. He had been the runt of the litter, and the original owners named him Cry Baby because he would tend to whine, if he didn't like something. Zeke didn't like being tied up. His pen was right outside the bedroom window, and he decided to whine until he was untied. It was summertime, and the windows were open. Ron could not get to sleep with all of that whining. He blurted out to the dog, "I wish you were dead!" As soon as those words came out of his mouth, Ron reached his arm out to grab them before they could get away. He immediately told God, "I am sorry, and I didn't mean to say those words." Zeke died within a week. What if that happened in our lives? What would we say that we would regret?

"For we all stumble in many things. If anyone does not stumble in word, he is a perfect man, able also to bridle the whole body" (James 3:2)

In the next verses, the apostle James makes a powerful analogy comparing the tongue to the bit in a horse's mouth. The reigns connected to the bit enable the rider to turn the whole body of the great animal. He then adds a second analogy—that of the rudder on a ship. The relatively small plate at the stern is shifted by the steering mechanism to apply drag to change the direction of the ship. Then he writes, *"The tongue is a fire, a world of iniquity. It defiles the whole body. It sets on fire the course of nature and is set of fire by Hell"* (James 3:6)

We know the bridle is designed to enable the rider to control the direction of his horse, and a rudder steers a ship. These analogies illustrate the spiritual reality that the things I say with my mouth will profoundly affect my heart and my life. For example, if I gossip and criticize a brother behind his back, I will greatly affect my own attitude about him. The more I talk, the more my tongue steers my heart toward bitterness and even anger. By the same token, a commitment to speak positively about everyone will tend to make me a more positive and happy person. The things you do will not affect my attitude toward you nearly as much as the things I say about you. My tongue will profoundly affect my life as well as the lives of those who hear me.

The tongue is also a "fire." That is, the destruction caused by a few bitter or hateful words can continue to cause ongoing and all-embracing destruction to multiple lives as it spreads through a community. Words spoken may never be undone. Words, which cause wounds, destroy lives, or cause unimaginable hurt can never be erased. That is a sobering thought. Words have power, and once the fire of those words is out, the course of nature is that others will repeat and embellish those words, and the spread of the fire continues. How hard is it to bring our words under control?

But no man can tame the tongue. It is an unruly evil, full of deadly poison. With it we bless our God and Father, and with it we curse men, who have been made in the similitude of God. Out of the same mouth proceed blessing and cursing, my Brethren, these things ought not to be so. (James 3:8–10)

What does it mean to curse men? It is speaking anything about or to someone that isn't good or positive. It is destructive, tearing down, hurting, and malicious. The words have a devastating effect on others. Just speaking can have that negative effect on people. How often is sarcasm or "just joking around" really cursing and bringing harm into someone's life? Far too often. Only with the Holy Spirit's help can we tame our tongue.

Let no corrupt word proceed out of your mouth, but what is good for necessary edification that it may impart grace to the hearers. And do not grieve the Holy Spirit of God, by whom you were sealed for the day of redemption. Let all bitterness, wrath, anger, clamor (to shriek, cry out) and evil speaking be put away from you with all malice. And be kind to one another, tender hearted, forgiving one another even as God in Christ forgave you. (Ephesians 4:29–31)

According to the rules of standard English grammar, when no subject given in a sentence, the pronoun "you" is the subject of the sentence. Place your name in the beginning of these verses. "Jan, let no corrupt word proceed out of your mouth." "Ron, grieve not the Holy Spirit." "Linda and Martha, be kind to one another." That is for you to do. These are basic instructions for the body of Christ." Words are powerful. Let us continue to learn to speak edifying words so that rivers of living water can flow from us.

Chapter 2

Blessing and Cursing

Out of the same mouth proceed blessing and cursing. My brethren, these things ought not to be so. (James 3:10)

Do we understand the power of blessing and cursing? Obviously, this has been a problem throughout the church age, and particularly today. James said, "It shouldn't be so. The problem of speaking well and not speaking to hurt others is prevalent in our lives today." Why? Let's look at an example from the Old Testament, which may help us understand blessing and cursing.

Then the children of Israel moved, and camped in the plains of Moab on the side of the Jordan across from Jericho. Now Balak the son of Zippor saw all that Israel had done to the Amorites. And Moab was exceedingly afraid of the people because they were many, and Moab was sick with dread because of the children of Israel. So Moab said to the elders of Midian, "Now this company will lick up everything around us, as an ox licks up the grass of the fled." And Balak, the son of Zippor, was king of the Moabites at that time. Then he sent messengers to Balaam, the son of Beor, at Pethor, which is near the river in the land of the sons of his people, saying this: "Look, a people has come from Egypt. See, they cover the face of the Earth, and are settling next to me! Therefore please come at once, curse this people for me, for they are too mighty for me. Perhaps I shall be able to defeat them and drive them out of the land, for I know that he whom you bless is blessed, and he whom you curse is cursed. (Numbers 22:1–6)

After four hundred years of slavery in Egypt, the descendants of Israel (Jacob) were finally freed to return to their God-given homeland, Israel. As they were camped in the plain of Moab for a brief respite, right next to them the King of Moab was plotting their destruction. His weapon of choice was a prophet of God to come and curse the nation so that the Moabites might have a chance to defeat the nation of Israel. This is a fascinating account, concerning the power of words. Much of the time when I was reading about Balaam and his talking transportation, I only saw that the Lord could have a donkey talk. Yes, that is fascinating, but the reason behind the whole incident was the incredible belief in the power of the spoken word.

As you read this account, consider the power of your words. Truly, the power of blessing and cursing is in the power of the tongue. Imagine our words having the same effect on those who hear what we speak. Are we speaking blessings or curses?

The rulers of Moab gathered money and set off to hire the prophet Balaam to pronounce a spiritual curse against Israel. God came to Balaam and asked, "Who are these men?" Balaam explained, "King Balak sent them, and he (Balak) wants me to go with them to curse this people who have come from Egypt." And God said to him, "You shall not go with them; you shall not curse the people for they are blessed" Numbers 22:12.

So Balaam arose and told the elders to go back because the Lord refused to give him permission to go with them. When Balak heard this, he sent more princes to persuade Balaam to come to him and curse the children of Israel. *And God came to Balaam at night and said to him; "If the men come to call you, rise and go with them but only the word which I speak to you, that you shall do." So Balaam rose and went with them and God's anger was aroused because he went, and the Angel of the Lord took his stand in the way as an adversary against him.* (Numbers 22:20–21)

Three times the angel of the Lord stood before Balaam's donkey. The first time the donkey went into a field. Balaam hit the donkey. The second time the donkey hurt Balaam's foot, trying to squeeze past the angel of the Lord. Balaam struck the donkey again. The third time the donkey lay down. (He probably thought, This is enough. I can't get away from this guy.) Balaam struck the donkey for the third time. The donkey talked to Balaam. "Hey, why are you beating me? Haven't I always been a good donkey? Talk to the big guy with the sword." At that point, Balaam finally saw the mighty angel of the Lord, the one his donkey saw from the beginning. It is worth noting that Balaam's greed not only made him blind to a spiritual being standing right in front of him, but it made him oblivious to the fact that his donkey was doing the talking. Ultimately, it just doesn't pay to be a prophet who loves profit.

The angel said, *"Go with the men, but speak only the word that I speak to you."* Three times in three different places, altars were built, sacrifices were made, and three times Balaam blessed Israel. Balak, the king of Moab, built altars three times. To do that much work, he must have believed that the words Balaam spoke would come to pass. He knew the power of blessing and cursing. The Lord believes in the power of blessing and cursing. As such, he allows this impressive illustration of the power of words. He made Balaam's donkey talk with him and afterward revealed himself to Balaam with the warning, *"Only speak the words that I give you."* The illustration of having his donkey talk was complete with an evocative warning against careless words.

Imagine the Pentagon unveiling a secret weapon—a man who could speak the curse of God's destructive power on an enemy, or invoke the blessing of the Creator of the universe on a friend. The word ''curse' used in this story of Balaam means to malign or stab with words. Have you ever been stabbed in the back with words? Words that stab instead of bless are certainly not rivers of living water.

I've often experienced this in my own life, at work. I had been employed by a local company for four years, with over twenty-fve years of experience in the field. They asked me to get a commercial driver's license. I was willing and studied the material and prepared to take both the written and skills test. Before I took the test, the owner of the company came to me and said not to be disappointed or discouraged when I failed the exams because no one in the company ever passed the first time. When I passed the test on the first try, he was not happy about it at all.

In order to do certain work in a neighboring county, my employer needed a contractor's license. They had tried to pass the test and failed. Because a majority of my work experience took place in that county, I was familiar with the codes that were covered on the licensing test. I offered to review what was necessary and take the test for them. I passed, and the company received the license. Again, the owner was not pleased.

Not long after I started with the company, I was led by the Lord to start a church. We listed our times and location on the church page of the local paper. The day after the first appearance of our listing in the paper, the owner of the company came over to my vehicle while I was getting out, yelling, "You started a church! You! I just can't believe that." The words came out in such a harsh tone they seemed to imply disgust about my new venture. I was surprised and taken back because he was a Christian and a member of the Gideons.

From that time on, the owner had nothing good to say about me. I watched as everyone received yearly raises except me. New people with no experience were hired and started at a higher salary than I was making, and within a short time, I was working under them. I was experienced and did everything I could to help the company. I was very good at my job, but it seemed as if there were forces beyond my control trying to sabotage everything I did. It was discouraging and frustrating. I felt as though I was fighting against an enemy in the dark. I really didn't know what would come next and how to overcome this adversary.

I went to test some lines on a project and discovered a broken gauge. By the time the gauge was fixed, the day was over. The next day, I tested the lines and every line failed. I told the superintendent they had defective fittings in the lines. Only once before, in twenty-five years had I seen every line fail, and it was caused by defective fittings. The owner met me the next morning and went along as I tried to test the lines again. Around noon, he said to pack up and go to the shop. At the shop, he came over as I was getting out of the company truck and said, "We are going to call it quits."

"Okay," I said.

I wasn't sure what he was talking about. He kept talking but I have no knowledge of what he said for the next minute or two, because as he was talking—to my amazement—he began to shrink and take on toad-like features. I don't know how long that vision lasted. After watching this startling transformation, I realized that he was firing me. I think I said, "Okay," and then went inside to tell the general manager about the defective fittings on the project.

As I went outside to leave, several of my coworkers were finishing their lunch. As I said good-bye to them, they were all smirking except one young man. He stood up, extended his hand and said, "I want to thank you for all that you taught me. It has helped me a lot, and I want you to know I appreciate all you did for me." As he was speaking while shaking my hand, I watched him grow six to eight inches taller. I was stunned and in awe of what I saw.

The owner said that I cost him thousands of dollars by seeking to sabotage his lines. Actually, they discovered defective fittings on the lines that I wasn't a part of developing and they also detected some poorly executed installation work. The owner's words, spoken either to me or about me, affected my time and performance while I was under his authority in the work place. I prayed to understand what I saw when I had visualized the owner shrinking and taking on the features of a toad, and why the young man grew as he shook my hand and expressed thanks. The answer was this: "The quality and effect of their words affected their spirits. You are no longer under the power and authority of the words spoken against you."

I didn't understand completely at the time, but it certainly caught my attention about the power of words, especially those spoken against me.

The next company I worked for was distinctly different. I had worked for less than an hour when the general superintendent motioned for me to stop so that he could talk with me. His said, "You know what you are doing. You have a radio, if you need anything. I have other jobs to go to. I don't need to stand around and watch you. You are fully capable."

I was doing something, which the previous company had said I wasn't qualified to do. The next morning, the vice president of the company complimented me on my work based on what he heard about my ability. Everyone from the owner to new employees spoke well of me. For several years, I received the quality award for outstanding achievement (again doing what I was told I wasn't qualified to do previously)! It was the most rewarding and satisfying job experience, ever. Why? It was the power of the words spoken.

These experiences were object lessons in my life. I wasn't reading about or watching DVDs on the power of words. It was my life. I was living in the power and authority of words. I recently asked a friend, "How is your new job going?"

He replied, "I told my boss that I had lost my confidence in my ability to do the job." The comments from his boss had been consistently negative and critical. Instead of motivating him to measure up, the cutting and demeaning remarks had crushed his spirit. I knew exactly what he was going through.

How do you change a negative, caustic environment? How do we overcome criticism and negativity? Try this simple technique. I've watched it work for others and for myself.

When Christ sent disciples out by twos, he gave them this admonition, "Whatever house you enter, first say peace be to this house" Luke 10:5. I believe there is a truth and principle to saying, "Peace to this place." I don't believe that truth cares whether it is a house, a factory, or a retail store. We should speak peace into it. Another step is to pray immediately, if negative words or criticism comes at you. Pray that those words will lose their power and effect on you. Then ask for grace and peace to settle your mind and heart.

What is happening to the people around us because of our words? Do we speak peace to our work place? How about our children, our coworkers, and those with whom we interact during the week? Are there blessings of living water flowing from us or stabbing curses? The words we speak each day profoundly affect not only those that hear us, but our own hearts and lives as well.

Chapter 3

Complaining and Murmuring

After the great deliverance from Egypt, the nation of Israel wandered in the wilderness for forty years. That seems to be a very long time to be on a camping and hiking trip. Why did this journey take so long?

After the parting of the Red Sea and some journeying, the nation of Israel was finally on the threshold of the Promised Land. It was decided that they better check out the land. One leader from each tribe was chosen to spy out the land. The land of Canaan was a good land, a land "flowing with milk and honey" with an abundance of fruit. There was, however, a slight problem. Giants lived in the land. That should not have been a problem for the God who delivered them from the slavery of Egypt. The nation of Israel was just like the rest of us. When we focus on our situation and circumstances and not on our Almighty God, we do what they did, but I am getting ahead of the story.

Different Viewpoints

Ten of the twelve men who spied out the land thought it would be impossible to conquer because of the giants. They said, "We were like grasshoppers in their sight." Where did they get that hyperbole? The tallest man who ever lived that we have any evidence of was Goliath of Gath, who stood almost ten feet tall. Some of the men from the seven nations, inhabiting the promised land were tall, but they were not nearly that tall. It was their own imagination and spirit of fear that caused them to assume they were "grasshoppers in their sight."

Ten of the twelve men were focused on the giants who lived in the land, all the while only two, Joshua and Caleb, thought they should make preparations to take the land. Our perspective often dictates how we respond. It is fine to have differing viewpoints as long as they do not take us away from what God wants and is leading us to do.

"But the men that went up with him said, *"We are not able to go up against the people; for they are stronger than we are."* And they brought up an evil report unto the children of Israel."* (Numbers 13:31–32)

15

Note that the ten spies brought back an "evil" report. The information was essentially true, but it was considered evil because it focused on the flesh and did not inspire faith in the people.

The unbelieving spies used their words to convince the children of Israel that it would be impossible to possess the land. What did the children of Israel do? They lifted up their voices and cried. (Does this sound familiar?) There is nothing wrong with having emotions. They are part of us and make us who we are. There is no sin in having emotions, but what they did next was a problem. Many of us, or even all of us, have fallen into this scenario.

Murmuring
"And all the children of Israel murmured against Moses and Aaron" (Numbers 14:2).

The whole congregation said it would have been better if they had died in Egypt. The situation might not have looked good but complaining and murmuring has never and will never improve a situation. It was their murmuring, which brought God into action.

And the Lord spoke to Moses and Aaron, saying, *"How long shall I bear with this evil congregation who complain against me?? I have heard the complaints, which the children of Israel make against me."* (Numbers 14:26–27)

Isn't that interesting? The words they spoke were against Moses and Aaron. Nowhere in the story is it recorded that the children of Israel said anything against God; it was all against Moses and Aaron. However, when we complain against authority we are actually complaining against God. Do you mean that when I complain against my boss I am complaining against God? I do not have to say that; the Bible already states that. We should be thankful that God's grace is so abundant in our lives, or our lives might be totally different. But there are always consequences for our murmuring and complaining. How many blessings do we miss because of murmuring? I know I have missed too many, and I do not want to miss any more. I control that by choosing whether or not to murmur.

In Numbers 10, we read that Miriam and Aaron spoke against Moses. She openly disapproved of his latest marriage partner. The topic or source of our murmuring is not really as important as our murmuring response. Aaron and Miriam were the older siblings, but Moses was God's chosen leader for the entire nation and had greater spiritual and civil authority. Speaking against Moses in public was wrong, and God dealt with them accordingly.

"I speak with him face to face, even plainly and not in dark sayings; and he sees the form of the Lord. Why then were you not afraid to speak against my servant Moses?"(Numbers 10:8)

"And when the cloud departed from above the tabernacle suddenly Miriam became leprous, as white as snow" (Numbers 10:10)

Leprosy is a biblical type of sin. The sin in this story was the way they spoke against Moses. This was not just a sibling rivalry, and it probably wasn't done privately. In our lives, we will disagree with the choices of others. This would not be considered unusual. How we speak against or about the authorities, who are ordained by God, though will affect our lives. We may disagree with others, but we should also learn to do it reverently and with grace. Sometimes, the conflict we have in our lives may be traced back to how we have spoken against someone.

This story has a happier ending. Miriam was exiled from the camp for seven days, but she was healed and restored at the end of the seventh day. I praise the Lord for not judging us as harshly as that, but we can all learn a valuable life lesson from Miriam. What happens when we murmur and complain? Does it affect our lives?

Murmuring Affects Us

The anger and judgment of the Lord may seem to be demonstrated differently today, but the truth is still relevant. When we murmur or complain against spiritual authority, we are in a very real sense complaining against God. Miriam got a quick reality check when she complained against Moses. I am sure that becoming a leper would tend to get anyone's full attention. Like me, you might be able to recall a few occasions in your life when a sudden attack of painful white skin would have been entirely deserved. We do not suddenly contract leprosy every time we dishonor spiritual leaders, but does that mean it is acceptable to God that we do so? When we complain against authority (against an employer, pastor, or parent) we are complaining against the Lord. We may not have the wisdom to understand that many of the troubles we have in our life are the direct result of murmuring against authority. Our complaints never affect those we complain against as much as they affect our own lives.

Paul wrote to Timothy and told him to pray for those in authority because it is spiritually beneficial for us. It is generally easier for us to understand the principle than it is to put it into regular practice. It is so tempting to complain.

Jesus therefore answered and said to them, "Do not murmur among yourselves." (John 6:43)

"Nor complain, as some of them also complained and were destroyed by the destroyer." (1Corinthians 10:10)

"Do all things without complaining and disputing." (Philippians 2:14)

Complaining Creates Discord and Hurt

The New Testament agrees with the Old Testament about complaining, but the grace of the New Covenant sustains us. I listed three verses from the New Testament, which include the words "murmur" or "complain." There are many verses in the New Testament, which describe or illustrate the various uses of words. Paul especially mentioned corrupt communication, evil speaking, foolish talking, blessing, and cursing. Our words of complaining, murmuring, evil speaking, corrupt communication and cursing have the power to create strife, animosity, friction, discomfort, and damage. This is true in the workplace, in personal relationships, in marriages, and even in friendships. The word of God tells us not to speak negatively about other believers. The words we speak should be good; they should bring blessings.

Do not speak evil of one another, brethren. He who speaks evil of a brother and judges his brother, speaks evil of the law and judges the law. But if you judge the law, you are not a doer of the law but a judge. (James 4:11)

The Greek word *katalaleo* is translated in the King James Version into the phrase, "speak evil." Sometimes, a believer will say, "No, it's not evil, because it's the truth." The word "evil" simply means that the effect of the words is harmful, whether they are true or not. When we damage the reputation of other Christians, we are speaking evil of them. The Bible clearly teaches that if we have anything negative to say about another believer, we should go to them in private and resolve the issue, rather than spread gossip and cause others to take up offense.

For example, a Christian wife may be upset with her husband, feeling hurt that he is not meeting her needs in some way. In speaking to her unsaved sister she pours out her heart about her pain and disappointment. The sibling naturally sympathizes with her, and she feels better. But suppose the Lord had planned to use that husband to lead the sister-in-law to salvation. That person will never be able to receive the gospel from him because she has picked up an offense against him.

Why is it important to refrain from complaining, or murmuring, or speaking evil? It is important to choose our words carefully because our words have power. Words may hurt the feelings of everyone involved. Words may destroy friendships or ruin marriages. The effect of words may last a lifetime and inhibit our ability to grow and function the way Christ desires us to function. It is true for earthly relationships; it is also true for spiritual relationship within the body of Christ and it may affect our relationship with our Lord.

Do Our Words Stab Others?

One meaning of integrity is wholeness. If you are an integral part of a company you are a vital and functional part of the company. Are we really whole? Are we complete, or are we only partially whole? The word "curse" from the story of Balaam carries the idea of stabbing with words. If I were to be physically stabbed repeatedly, I would bleed and possibly die. Even if I survive the attack, I would suffer extensive pain and retain scarring for the rest of my life. The effect of words on our souls and spirits is just as damaging and most of us have the scars to prove it.

What is the lasting result of stabbing words? When the owner of the company I wrote about in "Blessing and Cursing" chapter spoke against me, I was stabbed in my soul. Complaining behind the back of another believer is like an emotional stab. How many saints in the body of Christ or in the world are spiritual zombies? They are functioning to a point, but have no power, no joy, and no spark in life. Their lives carry the essence of death. They are wounded and immobilized emotionally and spiritually. How many Christians do not attend any fellowship because of the wounds or stabbing they had received from other believers?

Words have the power to wound but they also have the capacity to bring healing.

Heaviness (anxiety or wounds) in the heart of man causes depression but a good word makes it glad. (Proverbs 12:25)

A soft answer turns away wrath. (Proverbs 15:1)

A wholesome tongue is a tree of life but perversion in it breaks the spirit. (Proverbs 15:4)

This applies to the one speaking *and* the one listening.

A man has joy by the answer of his mouth and a word spoken in due season how good it is. (Proverbs 15:23)

The heart of the wise teaches his mouth and adds learning to his lips. Pleasant words are like a honeycomb, sweetness to the soul and health to the bones. (Proverbs 16: 23–24) If we speak well, we will be healthier and happier.

Death and life are in the power of the tongue and those who love it will eat its fruit. (Proverbs 18:12)

What is the effect of your words in your life? Do you have ease or disease? Do your words give sweetness to the soul and health to your bones? Complaining may bring disease into your life. Our lives will never be what they could or should be, if we habitually pout instead of praise.

We Should Reject Words That Aim To Hurt Us

When Christ sent the disciples out in pairs, they were told to invoke peace on whatever house they entered, and if their peace would not abide, there they were to shake off the dust from their feet and move on. Shaking the dust off was a physical act, but it was saying that they would have nothing to do with that place. It also symbolizes the refusal to let the rejection hinder our joy and faithful service to the Lord. Sometimes, we need to shake off the words that are spoken against us. I recommend speaking our resolution out loud. "I do not accept those words, and they will not affect me. I pray and ask for deliverance from those words and they are to be discarded from my life, my mind, and my spirit. I pray those words would fall to the ground, dry up into dust, and blow away."

Often, I find the need to say aloud, "I forgive them," as a godly response to the words, which have been spoken against me. Whenever I feel as though something someone has spoken is "getting under my skin" and is affecting my life in some way I know, I must ask for forgiveness. My speaking releases the power and authority of the Holy Spirit to set me free. When I don't forgive, it is like putting a stone in each shoe; it is going to be an irritation. Inability to forgive will keep my mind focused on the irritation. Forgiveness always produces freedom. At times, I may feel slighted or wounded by negative words. I have learned to speak about forgiveness to the person who spoke the words. They may not have asked for forgiveness; they may not even know the effect their words had on me. By forgiving them and rejecting their words I am free. When I do not forgive, I allow their words to assault my freedom, attack my mind, and become stones in my shoes.

Are there any areas of your life where complaining, either by you or against you, is trying to rob you of your peace? Are there wounds in you, or do you cause wounds in others? Do you need to ask for forgiveness, or do you need to forgive others? Complaining is harmful to you and to those who hear you. Don't think that just because everyone complains, it is justified or excusable? Murmuring is destructive to you and to those who hear. In the next chapter, I will share some insights on thanksgiving. The giving of thanks to God is the clear living water contrasted to the polluted river of complaining.

Chapter 4

Learning To Overcome With Thanksgiving

Complaining is not just murmuring, "bellyaching," being crabby, or saying something against authority. It is using your words to open a multitude of complex adversities in your life on multiple levels. It may affect you physically by causing stress in your soul by repeatedly being negative about a person or situation. Complaining affects your soul and body, not only by the chemicals secreted by various glands, but by the dark thoughts and emotions stirred up in your mind as well. Murmuring (grumbling) and complaining will bring sorrow to your spirit. Your spirit, and the Holy Spirit are grieved by your murmuring.

There are numerous verses in the Bible that give us direction about the way we should speak on specific situations. Why did the Holy Spirit inspire so much divine instruction on the use and misuse of the tongue? Perhaps we need to be reminded in many different ways to watch how we speak.

Therefore put away lying, let each one of you speak truth with his neighbor for we are members of one another (that sounds simple until you consider little deceptions, half-truths or maybe just omitting part of the story and it is all lying),... *Let no corrupt communication proceed out of your mouth, but what is good for necessary edification, that it may impart grace to the hearers.* (Ephesians 4:25, 29)

We should not have anything bad, evil, or hurtful, which is spoken, but that which is good for necessary edification. That means we have a responsibility to speak in such a way that when someone needs to hear something good we are able to speak to them?

It also means we should be so careful, so guarded, about how we speak that our words are never corrupt.

"Let all bitterness, wrath, clamor (loud talking, crying out) *and evil speaking be put away from you with all malice. And be kind to one another, tenderhearted, forgiving one another, even as God in Christ forgave you."* (Ephesians 4:31–32)

"Neither filthiness nor foolish talking nor coarse jesting, which are not fitting but rather giving of thanks." (Ephesians 5:4)

"Let no one deceive you with empty words, because of these things the wrath of God comes upon the sons of disobedience." (Ephesians 5:6)

"Do all things without murmuring and complaining." (Philippians 2:14)

"Now this I say lest anyone should deceive you with persuasive words." (Colossians 2:4)

These verses tell us not to lie, speak truth, and let nothing corrupt but that which is good to edify and impart grace. Watch and do not let your speech be with any bitterness, wrath, and loud and coarse jesting (joking around), but let it be thankful and continually give thanks. There are two verses about being deceived by words and another tell us we should do all things without murmuring and complaining; all things means all things and so there is never a reason to complain.

"For with the heart one believes unto righteousness and with the mouth confession is made unto salvation." (Romans 10:10)

It is the mouth, the confession, the words spoken that activate the grace of God. Paul spoke to a young woman with a spirit of divination and the spirit came out of her (Acts 16:18). Our words affect the spirit world around us; when we confess to Jesus, the Spirit world takes notice that we are changed. When Paul spoke to the spirit of divination, it left; that means the spirit world is affected by our words.

Every Sunday words are spoken from thousands of pulpits. Those words affect those who hear; they influence the community and the spirit world. Our words are not just a specialized noise coming from our mouths; they are tools and weapons and a force of righteousness in our area of influence. Our words have the ability, the force and the power to change our world. How we choose to speak will bring good or bad consequences into our lives and the lives of others. It is our responsibility to choose how we speak, and it is more important than most of us realize.

Guide To Help Us Overcome Our Negative Talk

I shared my experiences at two different jobs; the words spoken to me and about me were vastly different. The environment was the result of the words spoken. How do we change the way we talk? How do we deal with negative or harmful words spoken to us?

Changing the way we speak begins with the understanding of how powerful our words are and also looking for biblical guidelines to bring into our lives. Effectively dealing with harmful or negative words spoken to or about us begins with speaking forgiveness to the people who spoke the words and praying that the words will have no effect on us. One important part of edifying and healing speech habits is giving thanks. Apostle Paul exhorts us to give thanks twice in the fifth chapter of Ephesians. Verse four says there should be no foolish talking but rather the giving of thanks. Verse twenty then tells us we are to give thanks for all things to God the Father in the name of the Lord Jesus Christ. There is more power in giving thanks than we can imagine. It releases us to surrender to the Lord and allow the Spirit to move in our lives.

I believe there are patterns in scripture that are formulas, which if we follow, will guide us to a better understanding of truth and make the reality of truth change our lives. Tis passage is a good example: *Rejoice always, pray without ceasing. In everything give thanks; for this is the will of God in Christ Jesus for you. Do not quench the Spirit. Do not despise prophecies. Test all things; hold fast what is good.*(1 Thessalonians 5: 16–21)

Rejoice

The word *chairo* means to be full of cheer, to exude gladness. The Lord is worthy of our praise, and rejoicing is the perfect response to his presence. Rejoicing always gives us a different perspective. A focus on self and people is the essence of unbelief, and it results in discouragement and depression. Conversely, a focus on God and his kingdom results in joy and rejoicing. If we always rejoice, there is no incentive to complain. To rejoice always is to cultivate a positive attitude, to look for the good in everything. Life lived in communion with God is a delightful adventure. Happiness is a choice, and the tongue is a rudder that can steer us toward joy and away from discouragement.

Pray Without Ceasing

If we are praying without ceasing, there is not a whole lot of time left to speak evil. Now this does not mean that we must spend our entire day on our knees or in a church meeting. It does mean that we are living with a continual awareness of God's presence, and that we are interacting with him in our spirit and listening to His small voice to guide us along. in everything, give thanks

Does this mean I should thank God for everything? I do not see a lot of exclusion clauses in this verse. It seems a little unnatural and strange to give thanks for the good, the bad, and the ugly. Why would the Lord want us to do this? What happens when I complain instead of give thanks? I am saying that I don't believe this will work for my good and my complaining is saying I do not believe God is going to help me in this situation. It is a negative faith brought forth by my words. It is saying I do not believe God is going to do anything about this. I have found when I am complaining that the Lord has to wait until I am finished before he can and will move. When I give thanks, I am acknowledging my limitations and putting every care and situation into the hands of my Lord so that he may do whatever he chooses. In my life, complaining stops God from moving. Giving thanks and getting myself out of the way allows God to move.

Do Not Quench The Spirit
By rejoicing, praying, and giving thanks, we allow the Spirit free reign to rule and move in our lives. However, if we choose to dwell on criticism, arguing, and complaining, we may inhibit the moving of the Holy Spirit throughout our lives.

Do Not Despise Prophecy
In rejoicing, praying, giving thanks, and allowing the flow of the Holy Spirit through our lives, we open our hearts to words of edification, exhortation, and comfort. Valuing the words of knowledge and prophetic utterances that are given by the Spirit demonstrates our respect and love for God himself. The word "despise" here does not mean to hate or dislike. It means to count something as insignificant. In Hebrews 12, the writer says that Jesus "despised the shame...for the joy that was set before Him." In other words, he considered the public humiliation of being crucified in public in just a loincloth as nothing compared to the eternal joy of heaven, and the company of millions of redeemed saints who would be with him because of his suffering and death.

Test All Things

Be sure all things line up with the word of God. Make sure they are right and true. Every prophetic word must be consistent with the written Word of God, the Bible. All teaching and preaching must be evaluated in the light of the scriptures. If someone prophesies something that does not come to pass, it is a false prophecy.

Hold Fast To That Which Is Good

I am going to put away negative words; I will hold tight to what is good and hold it up to the light of God's word.

I believe these preceding verses are godly principles, which, if we apply to our lives, will help us overcome our tongue. They will work in our lives, if we allow them room in our lives. These guidelines are not exact answers to every situation but are a help to us.

My Experiences and Failures

Experience has taught me how well these principles work. At one time I had a coworker who was deliberately sabotaging a machine I was running. He would go out of his way to make sure it was dirty. His actions were more damaging to me than to the machine. I complained to my boss and anyone who would listen. Nothing changed. I did everything I could to limit his access to my machine, but that was not always possible. He knew that what he was doing bothered me and so he would go out of his way to do more and more. (I have never understood that attitude.) I had known about the principles of rejoicing and giving thanks. I just wasn't following or using them.

One weekend, I was reading these verses and thought, Well, I haven't used them, have I? I rejoiced and gave thanks to God for the situation and for the grief it had caused me. I decided to rejoice and praise God and give thanks and not complain about the situation or about my antagonist any more. On Monday, when I went to work, another worker came up to me right after I walked through the door and said, "Did you hear that [my antagonist] had given his two-week notice and is leaving?" After a year of complaining and trying to find a solution, I discovered that giving thanks to God did immediately what I couldn't accomplish in a year of trying. I am not saying that every situation will immediately have results. I am saying it happened that way in my life.

A year later, another conflict arose. I am pleased to say I didn't take a year to rejoice and give thanks. It began on a Monday, I immediately rejoiced and gave thanks and on Wednesday that person gave his notice. He left on Friday and never came back. The truth was so dramatic and immediate that I knew it was the Lord's doing. Will it always work that fast? I would say probably not. I have rejoiced and given thanks for other situations where I didn't see any external results in six months, but my grateful heart kept me from bitterness and defeat. The benefit was internal, but very real. I believe in the truth of God's Word regardless of how long it takes to see the results.

I hope and pray that these first four chapters have added to your understanding of the power and effects of our words. When we rejoice, pray, and give thanks, we are saying positive words to release power into our lives. I believe the body of Christ needs to step up and take responsibility for the way we speak. Diligently—and armed with knowledge that our words have power—we should attempt to follow the biblical guidelines to make our words good and acceptable to others and to our Lord.

"*My people are destroyed for lack of knowledge. Because you have rejected knowledge I also will reject you from being priest for me.*" (Hosea 4:6) The word "destroyed" in this passage carries the meaning of to be utterly at a loss. How many lives are in despair today, because they a lack of knowledge of the power and importance of how we speak? The knowledge and understanding of our words, the way we speak and the authority of our words will change our lives and the lives of those we speak to, if we put into practice what we learn from these verses.

Our words have power and because they do we should learn how to use the weapon of our words to do good and not evil. We need to remove our wrong patterns of speaking and let rivers of living water flow from us.

Part II

The Function of Prophecy

Prophecy should function in our lives. How is that to function or become real in our lives? We should learn to eliminate the murmuring and complaining in our lives, and the next step is to allow our words to be positive to those who hear us. By speaking those words, they may be words of encouragement or, under the inspiration of the Holy Spirit, they become prophecy. This section looks at the biblical guidelines for the use of prophecy and how we may learn to allow it to become a blessing in our lives.

Chapter 5

First Corinthians Thirteen: The Love Chapter

The Importance of Love

Portions of 1 Corinthians 13 are some of the most quoted verses in the entire Bible. Verses four through eight have been printed on cloth and parchment, framed, quoted in marriage ceremonies and preached from the pulpit. That is good. Each of us needs love and also to be reminded how love is to be practiced. We need to know the behavior of love, how it is shown, and how to make it real and active in our lives. Paul expounded on love in verses four through eight but prefaced his writing by stating it didn't matter what great things he had done; it didn't matter how great his faith was or even if he gave everything he owned to the poor. If he didn't have love all his greatness or good deeds would not profit him at all. He was stating that love had to be the foundation of all he had done or would do. It is equally important for us to learn to start from the foundation of love. Love, the love that Christ gives us, should be the fuel that energizes our every action. Imagine standing in front of the Lord and everything we ever thought, said, or did, which was not motivated by love, being thrown into a fire. Would there be enough left of our lives to prove we learned how to love?

The Definition of Love

Tis powerful chapter contains descriptions of love, but not a definition. There are numerous Greek words for love. The most commonly used are *eros, phileo,* and *agape.*

Eros speaks of physical love, and is a function of the flesh. *Phileo* refers to brotherly love, or friendship, and is a function of the soul, the mind, will, and emotion. *Agape* refers to selfless covenant love, and is solely a function of the spirit. This explains John's proclamation that genuine agape love is limited exclusively to those who are born of God. *"Beloved, let us love one another: for love is of God; and every one that loveth is born of God, and knoweth God. He that loveth not knoweth not God; for God is love."* (1 John 4:7–8)

An unsaved person may make friendships. He may even be in infatuation with a woman's beauty and grace, but he cannot love in the purest sense, because the sinful nature that rules his soul is selfish to the core. Love is giving. Love is being more concerned with the needs and feelings of others than with those of self.

Verses Four Through Eight

Love suffers long and is kind. That is, love is patient, gentle, and understanding. When people, events, and circumstances go against our plans, needs, or desires, are we patient and kind? Love is kind; love is nice to others, even when we are hurt by their actions. Love invests in the lives of others to help them through trials and tribulations with a strong stable influence. Do we really love?

Love does not envy. Do we have the ability to rejoice and give thanks when others seem to be more blessed, have more, and seemingly get ahead so easily while we choke on the dust of disappointment? Envy is no stranger in the body of Christ. "Why does the pastor want that person to lead worship instead of me? I'm a much better singer." "Why is she the head of the Sunday school?" What is actually being said? In reality, the disgruntled believer is saying, "I believe in me. I want to be important and recognized. I am more qualified; look at me." Love rejoices in the fortune of others and their blessings from God.

Love does not parade itself. Love does not try to draw attention to itself or its actions. It does not wave a banner to draw attention to itself. Do the skin cells on your arm say these things? "Look at me. I do a fantastic job of covering this part of your arm. I help you to feel warmth and cold, pleasure and pain, and you should notice. Why aren't you more appreciative of the job I am doing? Compliment me and build me up." Love does not strive to bring attention to its needs. The body is more important than the individual. To the genuine believer, God and other people are more important than the self.

"Let nothing be done through strife or vainglory; but in lowliness of mind let each esteem other better than themselves. Look not every man on his own things, but every man also on the things of others." (Philippians 2:3–4) Love does not behave rudely. Love is considerate of others. Love does not seek its own but cares for others and is not easily provoked. Love does not allow the petty actions of others to change who they are and how they respond. Love thinks no evil. That is, it does not dwell on the negatives about other people. Love is realistic without quick judgment of others and is focused on the love, grace and goodness of God.

Love does not rejoice in iniquity. It is never right to celebrate a wrong. Love rejoices in the truth. Truth is one of the most relevant factors in our lives. It is foundational. God's word is truth. Jesus Christ is truth; that is the foundation of love.

Love bears all things, believes all things, hopes in all things, and endures all things. I thought I was doing okay until I came to this passage. I do not always bear things well, and I am not sure I endure all things well. Actually, I am almost positive I could use some improvement in most of these areas. I can justify my actions or find excuses, but I know I fail more often than I like to admit. When we compare ourselves to what we should be and if we are honest with ourselves, we realize that without the grace and help of our Lord we will all fall short of the lofty requirements of love. Sometimes, I wonder if I would even get a passing grade in an agape love test.

A New Commandment

Christ told his disciples that the world would know they are his disciples *"if you have love for one another."* (John 13:35) In fact, right before he made that statement, in verse 34, he said, *"I have a new commandment to give you. You love one another as I have loved you."* He didn't say all would know they were my disciples, if they established a large church, feed the homeless, or provide for the poor and needy. None of these accomplishments will show you are his disciples. The United Way, Red Cross, and other organizations may do these things better and more efficiently than His disciples, but they may be motivated by greed. To some, charity is a lucrative business. However, if we want others to know we belong to Christ, we must be motivated by love for one another.

How are we to love one another? We are to love in word and deed. Do our words show love for others all the time? Or, are there little cutting, stabbing words such as the following? "I can't believe she wore that dress." "He isn't really very good at being a deacon, is he?" "They should find somebody else to do that job." Do we stab subtly with our words, or do we have rivers of living water flow from us as we bring blessing to others?

31

The Holy Spirit led Paul to include this passage on love between the introduction of the supernatural gifts in chapter twelve and the teaching on the unity of the body and the directives for their use both privately and corporately in chapter fourteen. The church at Corinth needed to be reminded of the importance, necessity, and beauty of love. It was important then, and it is vital for us today.

I have pondered the reasons why the Holy Spirit led Paul to expound on love in this passage. Why here? I am sure the truth of love is so universal that it could have been part of any of his writings. The chapter begins with "Tough I speak with the tongues of men and angels but have not love I have become sounding brass or a clanging cymbal." Paul is emphasizing the importance of love between the teachings on the spiritual gifts and their function in the believers' meetings. When Paul wrote this letter to the church at Corinth, it was without the chapter and verse designations we are accustomed to reading. There were no breaks or separation in the thoughts and themes he was conveying. This church needed to practice love, and it is the same for us. What if Paul was trying to teach not just the importance of selfless motives, but also about the practical application of the ethics of love? The last verse of the preceding chapter says, "Earnestly desire the best gifts and yet I show you a more excellent way."

A More Excellent Way

Chapter fourteen begins with *"Pursue love and desire spiritual gifts, but especially desire the gift of prophecy."* The teaching I have heard separates love from the introduction in chapter twelve and the instruction of how the gifts function in the corporate body. Since there were no chapter breaks, we can reasonably infer that the thoughts should be blended together in perfect harmony and balance between the gifts, the motive prompting their use, and their practical applications. Love is the basis or foundation of using the gifts. When Christ opened the eyes of the blind, healed the man with a withered arm, and healed the woman who was bent over, were those just a manifestation of the gifts or an expression of the love of the Father? Were they just tools so that Jesus could expound some great truth, or were they the expressions of the love of God flowing to those in need?

What if Paul was saying not only to desire (to have zeal, or passion for) spiritual gifts but also to allow God's love for others to flow through us in such a way that the function and operation of those gifts become a normal part of our lives? Is it possible that the body of Christ has to mature and realize that to truly love the way Christ loved, the way he told his disciples to love, and the love Paul talked about is for us to have a desire to prophesy and to allow his love to flow through us by way of the gifts? It seems to me that I have read something about, "You have not because you ask not." It is real and available, but are we willing to ask? Are we willing to love the way Christ loved? Do we have a zeal and passion to use the gifts of love?

In October of 2011, the midweek service for the first week consisted of two couples and myself. A young woman, Crystal, was in a serious auto accident in 2005 (her testimony is in the back of this book). For years after the accident, she was confined to her bed and a wheelchair and was severely limited in both movement and ability. A chiropractor said he would try to help but could give no guarantees. His treatments helped her so much that she was finally able to tie her shoes and walk, but she still had pain, weakness, tingling, and muscle spasms. She endured that for another two years.

On the night of our small group meeting, she was having a hard time. She was in severe pain and asked if we could pray for her. I was teaching about the gifts and also about the value of praying for one another. Her husband and another couple laid hands on her and anointed her with oil. The day was the seventh of October. When she came to the Bible study on October fourteenth, she said she wanted to do something before we started. She did a cartwheel. She had no pain, and to this day, she is working on a productive job. That was impossible before that night because if she worked at something for even a few hours it would take her days to recover. She was totally healed. Was this just some gift in operation or the love of God manifested through the gifts?

If we, the body of Christ, do not earnestly desire the spiritual gifts how many hurting people will miss the love of God being brought into a physical reality? For Crystal, the love of God as well as his healing grace was evident that night and every day since.

What is our desire? Do we desire to have rivers of living water flow from the Holy Spirit through us? Do we have a passion or a burning desire to see lives transformed by the love of the Father and his Son Jesus flowing through gifts and especially prophecy?

Chapter 6

What Is Our Desire?

Chapter twelve of 1 Corinthians ends with this statement: "But earnestly desire the best gifts; and yet I show you a more excellent way." It might benefit our understanding if we read it this way. "You should earnestly desire the best gifts. Yet, you should be motivated by love, which is the only true foundation for these gifts to operate."

Verse one of chapter fourteen admonishes us to pursue love. We are to follow, actually chase after, love like a hunter seeking prey. We are to seek to fulfill love and have the attributes of love listed in 1 Corinthians 13 guide our usage of the gifts. We are to desire spiritual gifts. We are to be zealous about and have a passion and burning desire for the gifts. We should have an eagerness and intensity for spiritual gifts and especially to prophesy. "Especially" here means chiefly, foremost, or to a greater degree. The desire to prophesy should be at the top of our lists of priorities.

Paul made it clear that we are to desire spiritual gifts, and in verse thirty-nine, he writes, *"Therefore brethren, desire earnestly to prophesy, and do not forbid to speak with tongues."* I do not believe this verse was included because he couldn't think of anything else to write. Did the Holy Spirit direct Paul to place a big exclamation point in this passage so that we would see the importance of prophecy?

The instruction is to desire spiritual gifts, but especially to prophesy. That puts prophecy to the forefront. We are not to desire gifts just for the sake of having gifts to talk about but to be yielded to the Holy Spirit so that he can speak words of encouragement through us to our brothers and sisters in Christ. We are commanded to use spiritual gifts, especially the gift of prophecy, so that rivers of living water may flow from the Holy Spirit through our innermost beings to give life to the body of Christ and also give light to a lost and wounded world.

If I gave you a gift of the latest, warp speed computer, and you left it in the shipping box sitting on the floor, what good would it be to you? You would have the gift, but what good would it be doing in your life? You would miss all the benefits you could have by not using the gift that was given to you. Paul wrote that we could all prophesy one by one that all may learn and be encouraged. The gift is available, but are we willing to use it?

Why did Paul place a great emphasis upon having a desire to prophesy? Is this gift greater than any other? Is it greater than the working of miracles, or faith, or the gifts of healings? The emphasis is there but why is it there? I believe it is because there is a greater need in the body of Christ to be edified, exhorted, and comforted. Also, there are multitudes of unsaved people who need to hear the gospel, but most will not respond to tracts tossed at them on the street. They are far more likely to respond to a conversation with a Spirit-filled believer who has a word of knowledge that can demonstrate he knows something about them that only God could have shown him.

We may not need miracles and healing every day, but in my life, I can become so spiritually drained that I need to be exhorted, edified, and comforted. Prophecy changes us on so many levels. It may affect our thinking, our emotions, and our spirits. Prophecy is a river of living water. Do we really want that river of living words to flow from us?

But he who prophesies speaks edification, exhortation and comfort to men. He who speaks in a tongue edifies himself, but he who prophesies edifies the church. I wish that you all spoke with tongues but even more that you prophesied; for he who prophesies is greater than he who speaks with tongues unless indeed he interprets that the church may receive edification. But now, brethren, if I come to you speaking with tongues, what shall I profit you unless I speak to you either by revelation, by knowledge, by prophesying or by teaching? (1 Corinthians 14:3–6) Verse three states that to prophesy is to speak to men to edify, exhort, and comfort. We are to prophesy both on an individual level and also on a corporate level. We are to speak to each other and sometimes to the church.

The result of obedience is blessing. The body of Christ needs to recognize the hurt and heartache of the world around us. Sometimes, we may have to quit texting, put down the iPads, turn off the mp3 players, silence our iPhones, and open our eyes and hearts to the people around us. We may have contact with others when we go to work, to the bank, to the grocery store, to the hardware store, or to restaurants. The opportunities are all around us if we will allow the Holy Spirit to guide and lead us.

I try to avoid making things easier for myself so that I will avail myself of more opportunities to make contact with people. For instance, I went into the local branch of my bank recently. A man whom I knew from another branch of the bank was there. We exchanged greetings, and I learned he was at this branch for training. While I was waiting for some change to be counted I felt impressed to say something more to him. I walked over to the cubicle where he was sitting and said, "I just wanted to tell you I appreciate your positive attitude and cooperation. Your friendliness is genuine, and I really appreciate that quality in you." He smiled and thanked me for saying that to him. His expression said more than his words. Those words touched him deeply.

Later that day, I was driving, approaching a T intersection in the road where I needed to turn right. A young woman was standing along the road to my right holding a crude cardboard sign. I glanced toward her and read the words, "Single mother." The light was green and traffic was moving, so I couldn't read the rest of her sign. I turned the corner and wondered if she were a scam artist or someone who really needed help. I felt led by the Spirit to pray for her. As I did, I had the impression that I should go back and give her some money and talk to her.

I turned around and drove back. I had to park about half a block away from where she was standing. I gave her the money, and she started to cry. As she looked at me, I said, "I know you do not like being at this point in your life, but God sees your struggles, and you will not be at this point in your life for very long."

The tears were gushing, and she said, "I really hope so. I have been praying." She told me of some of the struggles she was having and needed to pay a utility bill to keep her electricity on. This was her last resort as the bill had to be paid that day. She also said a car went by and the occupants threw some change at her and yelled, "Get a job." She was hurt by the judgmental remark, but her day didn't end with the pain of those words. The Lord wanted her to hear some positive encouraging words. I gave her my phone number and told her to call if she needed any more help. I continue to pray for this woman named Dawn.

Again, I went into a bank and was impressed to say words of appreciation and comfort to two tellers. Both were visibly touched, and their faces lit up. I left, and as I got to my car, I was led to go back inside and say something to a young woman who was seated in the lounge, waiting to see a personal banker. I sat beside her and asked if I could say something to her. I spoke what I felt was from the Lord. It was simple and encouraging. Her face lit up. When the spirit of a person is touched, their countenance glows.

My desire is to prophesy, to speak God's words to people. Romans 12 tells us that we should prophesy according to the grace that is given us. The word charisma or gift refers to a supernatural impartation of strength, ability, and motivation to love and help others. Grace, *charis*, is the root word of gift. Grace is the divine influence on the heart, and its reflection in the life. The best expression of the dynamic of grace is found in Philippians. *"For it is God that works in you, both to will and to do for His good pleasure."* (Philippians 2:13)

Inspired words are both good and edifying. Let our words of grace be given according to our faith. We should have the desire to prophesy and put our faith into action. The need is great. Not everyone you meet will have a blessed life, and your words of obedience may be the best thing that has happened to them in a long time. Will you be obedient?

Most of us will never reach the stature of Billy Graham, Oral Roberts, or any of the many stalwarts of Christianity, but if we have the desire to prophesy to those we come into contact with, we will begin making an impact on our world. We will have rivers of living water flowing to others. Consider: "Let no corrupt communication proceed out of your mouth, but what is good for necessary edification that it may impart grace to the hearers." (Ephesians 4:29)

This passage may not have a direct connection to prophecy, but it tells us that our words should be edifying and impart grace to the hearers. Do your words have the capacity to edify those who hear them? When we prophesy the words are anointed. When we are walking in the Spirit, our words are flowing from the throne room of the Lord. We become instruments of blessing through his love and the Holy Spirit. Through our mouths, we impart life to those who hear us. We should not give out anything from our hearts that will damage or defile the hearts of those to whom we speak. Our words should always edify those who hear us. Our words should consistently be words of grace.

But above all these things put on love which is the bond of perfection and let the peace of God rule in your hearts, to which also you were called in one body; and be thankful. Let the word of Christ dwell in you richly in all wisdom, teaching and admonishing one another in psalms, and hymns, and spiritual songs, singing with grace in your hearts to the Lord and whatever you do in word or deed do all in the name of the Lord Jesus giving thanks to God the Father through Him. (Colossians 3:14–17)

Here is another set of principles:

• **Put on love**. The idea is to allow love to be like a cloak or jacket we put on so that it is always with us.

• Let the peace of God rule in your hearts. Keep out of your heart everything, which would not allow the peace of God to rule or govern your heart.

• **Be thankful.** Tis is neglected by many of us. It takes effort and dedication to be thankful regardless of anything else.

• **Let His word dwell in you:** Share with others in wisdom, teaching, and singing.

• **Do all in the name and authority of Christ.** Let your words and deeds be in line with his word, and do all things with grace and thankfulness.

• **Let his word live in you.** If you are full of His Word, when you speak His Word will flow out as a river of living water.

Chapter 7

For You Can All Prophesy

Therefore, tongues are for a sign, not to those who believe but to unbelievers, but prophesying is not for unbelievers but for those who believe. Therefore, if the whole church comes together in one place, and all speak with tongues and there come in those who are uninformed or unbelievers, will they not say that you are out of your mind? But, if all prophesy, and an unbeliever or uninformed person comes in, he is convinced by all, he is convicted by all, and thus the secrets of his heart are revealed; and so falling down on his face, he will worship God and report that God is truly among you. (1 Corinthians 14:22–25)

A good friend came to my house early one Sunday morning. I was on our back deck, drinking a cup of coffee and watching the sunrise. This was a friend of over thirty years; we had spent countless hours conversing over a wide range of subjects.

His first statement was, "Last Thursday, I told God I wanted him to take over my life because I haven't been doing a very good job of being in control of my life. I knew from our conversations that his mother had gone to church and was a believer, but I had never known him to show an interest in Jesus or his church. I listened as he went over the events of his life, which brought him to this decision. After an hour or so, I told him that I needed to get ready for the Sunday morning service. His response was that he was going to come to the service also.

A missionary couple was visiting that morning; they were making the final preparations to go to Africa as a part of Wycliffe Bible translators. In our services, we often take time to prophesy to visitors and new people. As we had some of both groups that morning, I said that we would start with my friend Brian.

"And thus the secrets of his heart are revealed; and so falling down on his face, he will worship God and report that God is truly among you." (1 Corinthians 14:25) I do not claim to know or understand the secrets or treasures of a heart or spirit and how they are moved, upon or

touched by prophecy. A woman in our fellowship spoke to Brian about God knowing his heart and what he yearned for. She told him that God sees the routine he goes through and how his heart cries. I was watching my friend Brian's reaction, and she hadn't said much before his tears were flowing. Everyone encouraged him and said something uplifting to him. There was no doubt the Lord had gently, tenderly, and lovingly touched his life deeply.

After the service, he made his way over to me. "How did she do that? How did she know the routine I have every night with God? She doesn't know me, and I don't know her. I have never met her, and I know she has never met me. How did she do that? How did she know?" he asked.

"Brian, that happened so that the secrets or treasures of your heart would be revealed as proof of God's love for you. This is what happens when the church or body of Christ is sensitive and willing to be used to prophecy. The Lord wants you to know he will never leave you or forsake you," I replied.

Several months later, he asked me if she ever spoke about what she said to him. I told Brian she didn't remember what she said but was being sensitive to how the Holy Spirit was leading her that day. "It wouldn't matter what she remembered. It wasn't for her. It was for you." Brian has since shared with a number of people how much it meant to him. It had a great impact on his life, and he felt she might remember because it made such an impact on him. Isn't that what should happen when new people come into our fellowship?

Brian's story is one example; it is not a unique or isolated experience. It is the normal flow of a service as we share with those who visit our fellowship. I wanted to use Brian's story because we are in contact with one another, which is not always the situation when others visit. More than one time, I have spoken to a visitor and said I felt the Holy Spirit was leading the service to meet their needs and show the love of the Father and the Lord to them. I have watched as they respond to the words or prophecies of our fellowship and know the Lord indeed loved and touched them with and through the words spoken.

"For you can all prophesy one by one that all may learn and all may be encouraged. And the spirits of the prophets are subject to the

prophets, for God is not the author of confusion but of peace, as in all the churches of the saints." (1 Corinthians 14:31–3)

"Therefore brethren, desire earnestly to prophesy and do not forbid to speak with tongues, let all things be done decently and in order." (1 Corinthians 14:39–40)

I have read and meditated on these verses frequently, seeking a greater understanding of what they mean and how they should function in the body of Christ in a believer's meeting. "For you can all prophesy one by one." Is that possible in a service? I had never been in such a service to witnesses that. Perhaps I hadn't been in the right place at the right time. However, there those verses were in black and white. I could rationalize them into nothing or spend more time praying and finding a way to make these verses real and active in our fellowship.

Chapter twelve of 1 Corinthians advises us to earnestly desire the best gifts. Chapter fourteen starts by telling us to pursue love and desire spiritual gifts, but especially that we may prophesy. Verse five once again stresses that you must prophesy. Verse thirty-one says we all can prophesy, and verse thirty-nine tells us to desire earnestly to prophesy.

That is one admonition to earnestly desire the best gifts and four times we are admonished to earnestly desire and seek after prophecy, and to see prophecy as the highest priority in our pursuit of these spiritual gifts. What other subject has such an emphasis repeated that often in forty plus verses? Maybe it is important; too important to ignore any longer. Maybe we should pray that the eyes of our understanding would be opened to the relevance of this in our lives and in our services. What a great blessing anointed prophecy is! Prophecy can be a river of living water from the Holy Spirit flowing through us to lift the body of Christ to a new level of understanding and touch a dry and thirsty world.

One Sunday, Dennis Kutchner, who was the executive secretary of Calvary Ministries International, was with us for the morning service. A young man spoke to him and said he felt he had a ministry of help. He had been a blessing to many churches and pastors. He ended by saying his ministry was like an umbrella of protection and covered many areas to strengthen others. The CMI logo at that time was an umbrella, covering a globe with the words helping and strengthening the local church. The young man had never met Dennis or had he ever seen the logo, but what he said encouraged Dennis at that time.

I have been blessed and continue to be blessed when I see and hear the edification, exhortation and comfort given by prophecy. It is so very real and precious. My desire is to see it become such a part of the body of Christ that untold numbers will share in the joy and blessedness.

By not murmuring and complaining, but speaking as the Holy Spirit leads us, we unlock one of the greatest treasures of heaven—rivers of living water flowing from us. I believe there are more benefits to prophecy than most of us have ever considered. The later chapters in this book will explore and explain some of the benefits of prophecy.

Chapter 8

How Then Is It

How We Started

In the next few chapters, I want to explain how we at Christian Fellowship got started and some of the passion that I have. Hopefully, this will help others who wish to travel down this path. I have found it to be a rewarding blessed journey and pray you will also.

How is it then brethren? When you come together, each of you has a psalm, has a teaching, has a tongue, has a revelation. Let all things be done for edification. (1 Corinthians 14:26)

This scripture seemed to jump off the page of my Bible one day. Something began stirring inside. My spirit was being drawn to see this verse come alive. When you come together, each of you, everyone has something to contribute; each and every one brings a psalm, a teaching, a tongue, a revelation, a prophecy, or a good word of encouragement. I added the last two, but I believe Paul was not listing everything that could be brought to a service, but suggesting merely that everyone should bring something good to a service.

I haven't seen how every service is conducted in different churches, but I was sure I had not seen this made real—a service where everyone contributes something. This was radically different from just walking into a church service, sitting down, singing and worshiping, giving in an offering, listening to someone share a passage and message from the Bible, greeting someone on the way out and driving home.

This was saying to me that everyone should be a participant in the service and not merely a spectator! Wait a minute. How is that going to work? What if they didn't want to participate? What if they participated for themselves and not the Lord, or not for his glory? It is easy to question and wonder how it will work. I started seeing our fellowship time (church service for some) as a table for the food of a banquet. If I bring forth a message, sermon or teaching, we have meat on the table. However, just having meat makes for a bland meal. We have to have worship. The praise and worship time is a side dish, probably mashed potatoes. If a singer ministers with a "special" song, and we have a vegetable dish, perhaps corn, peas, or green beans, that is enough to sustain us, fill us up, and keep us coming back for more.

But what if we added a salad of personal testimonies, an appetizer of brief teachings from different participants on life lessons the Holy Spirit led them through that week? Why not have a cherry pie (you may insert your own favorite pie) revelation topped off by prophecy ice cream? Tongues and interpretation are the cake and a sweet beverage, exhorting and edifying the celebrants. Now we have a feast fit for king's kids! Why settle for anything less than the very best the Lord has for us?

When everyone brings something for edification, how much greater is the service? How much more do we see the love of Christ manifested? How much closer to fulfilling the Lord's desire do we get? How does each person mature and grow in grace when presented with the opportunity to give and participate rather than just watch?

How To Begin

People tend to respond more readily to what they understand. It is difficult to respond to an opportunity or situation if we are not sure what to do or what is required of us. Imagine being a goalie on a soccer team with no one instructing you to stop the ball from going into the net. You might duck away from the ball coming at you. When you learn how to stop the ball, deflect it, and then get the ball back to your team, you are able to respond correctly. You may not be very skilled as goalie but at least you have understanding. Now, all you need is practice. Babies are messy, yet no one punishes them for creating stinky messes. Normally, Mom and Dad love them through the mess and watch them grow.

Each one who comes has a responsibility to bring something. The problem is that they may not know it. The majority of Americans attend church services to "get a blessing" or to be entertained, and the concept of gathering to give and bless is new to them. Teaching is the first step to becoming aware that just warming a seat isn't what the Lord requires. Gentle, repetitive, coaxing, and teaching allows the Spirit of the Lord to work in a person's heart to magnify and make real the truth of God's word. We didn't have everyone participate by bringing their blessing to the body immediately. Frequently, I would ask if anyone has anything for the service.

When understanding is communicated to the body of Christ, almost all believers who have the desire to please the Lord accept the challenge readily. They tend to grow into the responsibility of adding to the service by bringing something spiritual. (I refer to this as bringing your blessing so that others may be blessed.)

Over the years, in our local fellowship, plenty of mistakes have been made. Not everything was edifying or theologically correct, but each one put forth the effort to bring a blessing. There were times of correction and growth, times for complementing the body adding to a service, flowing with grace and blessing, and times of teaching and encouraging when some of them fell short of perfection in their responses.

I can almost hear someone thinking, "That won't work in our congregation because" (you may insert any excuse here.) What if the Lord is bigger than any excuse? What if you have to be willing to change how you view church? From my experiences, watching and being part of the service where everyone contributes is generally a rich and deeply satisfying experience.

In one service, after the worship time, our worship leader, Ron Hults, shared about the way the Lord was working in his life helping him overcome in an area he was struggling. Someone else shared what the Lord taught her from a similar but different struggle. A third person shared how hearing the struggles of others and the knowledge of how the Lord was moving and working in his life helped him gain confidence and patience in his life. Each one took ten to fifteen minutes to share. Although each was different, each testimony blended well with the others. I felt a great peace and thanked each one for sharing. I said that those three mini-sermons were better than what I prepared. I had nothing significant to add except a prayer to close the service.

Where We Are
Allowing others to bring their blessings and allowing the Holy Spirit the freedom to move and use each one brings life into the service. I am willing to allow blessings from others, but I also seek to ensure, as far

as possible, that everything is decently done and in order. There is a responsibility to teach and bring the body to maturity as outlined in Ephesians 4: *And he gave some, apostles; and some, prophets; and some, evangelists; and some, pastors and teachers; for the perfecting of the saints, for the work of the ministry, for the edifying of the body of Christ: till we all come in the unity of the faith, and of the knowledge of the Son of God, unto a perfect man, unto the measure of the stature of the fullness of Christ: that we henceforth be no more children, tossed to and fro, and carried about with every wind of doctrine, by the sleight of men, and cunning craftiness, whereby they lie in wait to deceive; But speaking the truth in love may grow up into him in all things, which is the head, even Christ: from whom the whole body fitly joined together and compacted by that which every joint supplieth, according to the effectual working in the measure of every part, maketh increase of the body unto the edifying of itself in love.* (Ephesians 4:11–16)

Briefly, the role of spiritual leaders is equipping, edifying, and bringing the saints into unity. Christian teachers help people to grow in their knowledge of Christ, and to grow in their understanding of the word so that they are not ensnared by false doctrines. They teach the importance of speaking truth in love, growing up in all things in Christ, and working together to edify the body. All aspects of the service are important and all should blend together. We bring the blessings; the Holy Spirit blends it all together.

One Sunday, a woman laid hands on and sang an anointed chorus over each person in the room. It was a great blessing. Each service is unique in one sense, yet the same atmosphere of love and grace prevails. At times, a couple will move and anoint others and pray over them. Sometimes, it will be done while we are worshipping, sometimes during our quiet time before the Lord, but always in order.

Occasionally, I will sense in my spirit that a person has a blessing to give but may not understand or know what is being asked of him or her. This happens if someone is to give a word in tongues and has perhaps never experienced that blessing previously. One Sunday, I was particularly impressed that a woman was to bring forth a tongue but she didn't know how to yield or allow it to come forth.

I asked her, "Would you do something for me?"

She was apprehensive and said, "I don't know; it would depend on what it is you are asking."

I replied, "We are here in the service. I would not ask you to do anything that would harm or embarrass you. I would not ask you to do anything the Lord would not want you to do. Will you do what I ask?"

"Yes, I will. I trust you," she replied.

I said, "I am going to ask you to pray out loud in your spirit language."

Her face showed that she wasn't very comfortable with my request, but she closed her eyes and began to speak in her spiritual language. After a few syllables, the sweetness of the Holy Spirit's anointing gave the assurance that he was ministering. After an interpretation, I used the example to teach others.

Not all things go as planned. I recently felt led to have another woman who was new to our fellowship bring a tongue for us. I asked if she would pray for the rest of the service in her prayer language. I meant for her to pray for the service, but I knew she was to deliver the blessing of a tongue. However, I said, "Pray for the rest of the service," even though I meant for her to pray the part of the service not yet done. She thought she was to pray for the rest of the service. I had to interrupt her to allow for an interpretation, or she would have prayed until the service was dismissed. I learned a lesson myself in communication.

There have been amusing incidents like the one in the preceding paragraph. We all experience times of correction and teaching. But the practice of 1 Corinthians 14:26 in our meetings has drawn the fellowship closer to each other and to the Lord. It is awesome watching and being a part of the Holy Spirit blending our gifts and directing our times together.

I am personally blessed frequently by our worship leader. He is a longtime friend and co-laborer. He has the freedom to interrupt the musical worship to share, pray, and be obedient to the leading of the Holy Spirit. Ninety-nine per cent of the time when he stops to share it is a prelude to or part of the message I have for that day. We never discuss the service or what I want from him. When you allow others to grow under the Holy Spirit's guidance, something wonderful happens. They grow under the Holy Spirit's guidance.

Where Are We Going?

As the body matures, the obedience is greater along with the blessings of gifts and the manifestation of God's love. We are striving to be stewards of his grace and blessings. We want more of Jesus in our fellowship and in our daily interactions with others.

Chapter 9

From Desire to Reality

But earnestly desire the best gifts. And yet I show you a more excellent way. (1 Corinthians 12:31)

Pursue love and desire spiritual gifts but especially that you may prophesy. (1 Corinthians 14:1)

I wish you all spoke with tongues but even more that you prophesied; for he who prophesies is greater than he who speaks with tongues, unless he interprets, that the church may receive edification. (1 Corinthians 14:5)

Therefore brethren, desire earnestly to prophesy and do not forbid speaking with tongues. (1 Corinthians 14:39)

For you can all prophesy one by one, that all may learn and all may be encouraged. (1 Corinthians 14:31)

Pursue and Desire

Paul wrote that we should earnestly desire the anointing and the ability to prophesy. He emphasized it repeatedly. I have attempted in the chapters "What Is Our Desire" and "For You Can All Prophesy" to show the importance of learning what prophesy is and of bringing that blessing into our services. Pursue love, and desire spiritual gifts; earnestly desire to prophesy.

What does it mean to pursue love? We cannot chase after what we do not know. What do we know about love? God is love. How does God want us to love others in the context of spiritual gifts and especially prophesy? What if we cannot truly love and reach out to someone (the way the Lord wants us to), until we learn to open ourselves and desire to prophesy?

According to the third verse of chapter fourteen, to prophesy is to speak about edification, exhortation, and comfort to others. Should we not have an intense passion to speak through prophecy to build others, to help them draw closer to the Lord, or bring comfort into their lives by speaking forth good words?

Take the First Step

The first step to fulfilling our desire to prophesy is to examine ourselves and our motive. Do we want to be admired by others for our spirituality, or do we really want to serve others in love? Do we desire to bring blessings to others, or do we want people to believe we are a great blessing? I believe the Holy Spirit had Paul place so much emphasis on prophecy rather than the other gifts listed in chapter twelve for these reasons:

• Prophecy flows into daily conversations easily. When we are seeking to love one another, speaking grace and kindness through prophecy is a river of living water from us to them.

• We are commanded to exhort one another daily. We need to be constantly encouraged to stay strong for the Lord. If we as believers need to be encouraged, how much more does a lost world need it? (Hebrews 3:13)

• When we pray to the Father to love someone with our words we are pursuing love. We desire to be an expression of God's love to them.

• Prophecy blesses others; sometimes on a surface, emotional level but sometimes prophecy ministers on a deep spiritual level.

• It is needed to keep the body of Christ healthy and reach those who are to be a part of the body.

Practice, Practice, Practice

It would be wonderful if each person's temperament, obedience, and sensitivity to the Holy Spirit allowed prophecy to flow whenever we wanted, but from my experience most of us need some training, teaching, and practice.

"For you can all prophesy one by one, that all may learn and all may be encouraged." (1 Corinthians 14:31)

A friend of mine told me that during one of his prophecy seminars, he told the participants to prophesy, and they did. I started by choosing one person on Sunday morning and having everyone say something they heard from the Holy Spirit to edify, exhort, or comfort that person. The next Sunday, I would choose someone else, and we would all say something to edify, exhort, and comfort that person. We learned together and grew together.

When a guest speaker was present on a Sunday morning, we would say something to edify, exhort, or comfort the guest speaker (and sometimes his wife). I refrained from always using the word "prophecy." To some, the word implies that they have to have some great insight and deep revelation to be allowed to contribute. We must understand that prophecy must originate with the Holy Spirit, but it does not have to be profound or impressive.

One day, it seemed to me that almost everything went wrong. I was feeling discouraged and sad. That evening a brother said to me, "I feel I am to say a word to you, but I don't have any great insight."

As he was speaking those words, I was thinking, "I just want someone to tell me I am loved."

Then the brother said, "The only words I have to say are, 'I love you, hang in there.'" Those words sent warmth and a renewing sense of purpose and being through my soul. They powerfully kicked the blues right out of my heart. He spoke six words and lifted my spirit. Prophecy does not have to be a long treatise. Six words encouraged and comforted me that night.

When everyone was comfortable with saying something to edify, exhort, and comfort one person, I would ask one person to speak to everyone who was present. It was an opportunity to fulfill the scripture that we can all prophesy one by one. It was practice.

The practice helped us grow to know the guidance of the Holy Spirit and to yield to the Spirit. One guest said he liked coming to visit because he received more than he gave. I believe that many who come to receive teaching and ministry learn that they can and should prophesy. It wasn't hard, but sometimes, it was difficult to get ourselves out of the way. It is okay to be imperfect, but we need to be willing to be a blessing.

One sweet sister took an hour to say something to edify, exhort, and comfort seven others in a mid-week Bible study. She wanted to do well, to do it right. She was nervous, and at times tearful, and her words were halting and sometimes ungrammatical. Each person learns and practices differently, but the end result is learning to bless and love others through rivers of living water flowing from and through prophecy.

Another woman asked if I would expect her to say something because it was her first time at a meeting. I said, "Yes, you will speak to everyone." She was concise and succinct. She shared with us for about two minutes and then sat down. These two examples illustrate the range of difference in not only the time taken to speak but also the difference in the personalities of the participants.

A Little Caution

What we say when we prophesy should edify, exhort, and comfort. Sometimes, for the sake of the patient hearers, we need to improve our presentation. I started speaking to a dear brother with these words: "Knowledge puffs us up, but love builds us up." To know when each is needed is wisdom from the Lord. We should seek to know what someone needs. He missed the exhortation because he thought I was saying he was puffed up with knowledge. I was trying to convey the idea that we should not puff others up with knowledge when they need love. We are not always perfect in our delivery.

We want the delivery to be perfect every time we speak, but it usually isn't. We need to accept the fact that our speaking in a believer's meeting does not have to be impressive or brilliant, and in fact, it rarely is. Does the word we hear from the Lord convey love along with edification, exhortation, and comfort? If it does, it is good enough.

Everything must be done in love, with love, and through love. Strive to edify, exhort, and comfort. We cannot and should not be directive in our prophecy unless we are functioning in the office of a prophet or a pastor. Phrases such as: you need to, you should, must not be part of how we speak edifying words. If someone needs to do something in response to what the Spirit is saying, remember that it is the work of Holy Spirit to bring them conviction. It is his job to convince, and our job to speak in love. For practice, we do not direct or attempt to tell someone what they should do.

And when he (the Holy Ghost*) is come, he will reprove the world of sin, and of righteousness, and of judgment.* (John 16:8)

And be ye kind one to another, tenderhearted,   forgiving one another, even as God for Christ's sake hath forgiven you. (Ephesians 4:32)

Go Tell Others

Christians should speak to edify, exhort, and comfort those with whom they interact in life. We seem to be using more technology to diminish or even eliminate face time with one another. If we are not careful, we will be trapped by technology in a social and spiritual void. No matter how wonderful the music or how great the preaching is, the television and internet church services will never replace the gathering together of the saints for worship and body ministry.

There is no precise formula for the perfect way to prophesy and whom to prophesy to when we interact with others. However, I use these guidelines:

• Do we desire to have the Lord Jesus Christ love others through us by using prophecy? Pray that his love will flow through us.

• I do not know what someone might need but the Holy Spirit does. Pray for guidance to know who to speak to and what words to say.

• Wait for the right time. It is easy for me to get ahead of the Lord or leave a place before opportunities arise. Pray for wisdom and understanding and boldness when necessary.

• Let everything be done through love. We are to glorify Jesus. Pray that we do not interfere through pride or have anything in us, which would lead others to focus on us and not on the love of Christ.

Part III

The Importance of Prophecy

Unkind or caustic words cause grievous wounds, which may linger long after the sound of those words, have faded into silence. I have a theory. If hateful or critical words can cause emotional and even spiritual wounds, then loving and encouraging words can be used to heal emotional and spiritual wounds. The word of God has many verses about the use or misuse of the tongue. All the verses should be put into practice in our lives. If the body of Christ learns to speak positive words and cut back or eliminate the negative words, the complaining, and everything damaging to others or ourselves, we will affect our world dramatically.

It is not merely learning to emphasize the good words and eliminate the destructive words, but learning and desiring to prophesy, which will bring the greatest change and blessing. Speaking right words affects the souls of men. Prophecy affects both the souls and spirits of men. Prophecy reaches into and touches the spirits of the hearers not only to edify, exhort, and comfort, but also to bring the wonderful presence and anointing of God into their hearts. Also, interacting with others on a spiritual level brings emotional healing. I believe this deep spiritual healing is necessary for the body of Christ to be everything the church, the bride of Christ, is to be before Christ calls us home. It is prophecy flowing as rivers of living water that will bring healing and life to a world in desperate need and to the church with needs almost as great.

This section should open our understanding of the deep spiritual significance of prophecy and of the healing effects of words spoken through prophecy. We need to gain a greater understanding of the benefits and necessity of prophecy. God has chosen to speak through us for our mutual edification. Our desire and passion for God's kingdom and his people should be multiplied exponentially. Prophecy in believer's meetings should flow as rivers of living water.

Chapter 10

The Innermost Part

"The words of a talebearer (slanderer, gossiper) *are as wounds and they go down into the innermost parts of the belly."* (Proverbs 26:22)

One commentary used the metaphor of the inner rooms of the belly. The words of a talebearer are as wounds that are hidden in our spirit. They are tucked away, out of sight, and most of the time beyond our understanding. But when a trigger event or circumstance touches that wound there is usually an explosion of emotion. That is our natural response to a wound in our innermost spirit. Much of the time, the wounds may not even be remembered, but the effects boil up when something triggers or causes us to feel pain associated with that wound.

A Childhood Adage

"Sticks and stones may break my bones but names will never hurt me." We have all heard that old proverb, but it is not in the Bible. In fact, it is not biblical at all. It is good for us to be strong enough to mentally shake the words away so that they have no effect on us, but the expression is false when we are weak or already wounded and knowingly but unwillingly accept the words spoken. Children do not always know how to deflect the sting and hurt caused by words. Sadly, often these words come from parents or close relatives—"You will never amount to anything," or "You just aren't trying. Why can't you be like your brother?" These are just two examples of statements, which may cause the words to go down into our innermost being. They wound the spirit.

Personal Experience

I grew up in a happy family with a brother, a sister, and cousins to play with. We were poor, and I often heard, "We can't afford that," or, "We do not have the money to buy that." I learned, long before I started school, not to ask for things because we could not afford them. I was too young to understand exactly what that meant, but I was sensitive to the agitation and discomfort, which was caused by asking, so I learned not to ask for anything.

When I started school, I couldn't see what the teacher would write on the blackboard. (Yes, I am that old.). My first grade teacher (to whom I am eternally grateful), moved me to the front of the classroom. I still couldn't see well, so when she wanted me to answer, she would write in large letters for my benefit. I learned to read, and she helped me throughout the year.

The teachers for the next three years were not so kind and understanding. I thought they were unkind in their actions and very unkind with their words. I will admit I talked too much and goofed around. I couldn't see what they would write on the board, so I occupied myself with whatever I could. When I would give a wrong answer to a question or problem written on the blackboard, it was not only wrong but so far off that the teachers would comment in a condescending negative way and usually everyone would laugh. I guess answering "George Washington" when the correct response was "ten" was too much for them to understand. According to them, I was just lazy, a troublemaker, and a very poor student.

Of course, the laughter and ridicule led to isolation. I really wasn't trying to be a smart aleck, but I had no idea how to answer because I didn't know what was written on the blackboard. When this laughter and ridicule was added to my small size and lack of confidence, I felt emotionally wounded. I never replied or had an answer for what was said to me. I imagine I tried the teacher's patience and was perhaps rowdy out of boredom. I never copied any notes from the board except at recess, but at times, the teacher would make me go outside.

The second, third, and fourth grades were nightmarish for me. There was ridicule, laughter, and plenty of hurtful names. One of the favorite taunts was "You're so stupid. The answer was right there." Another remark came on occasion: "You're so stupid. Everybody knew that answer." No, not everyone; just the people who could see it. Sticks and stones may break my bones, but the wounds caused by mocking and hurtful names last for years.

Toward the end of my fourth grade, the music teacher was writing material on the blackboard, which was to be on the final exam. I knew I was not doing well in the class. During the semester there were quizzes, and I don't know if I accidentally had any right answers, but I felt I needed to do well on the exam, or I would not pass. I was afraid I would be in the fifth grade and have to go into the fourth for music class.

I asked a girl who sat across the aisle from me if I could borrow her notes because I didn't have everything written down. As I copied her notes, I started to recognize music symbols that I had only heard about. The notes were very good. I studied and memorized those notes and I really tried to memorize the scales and treble cleft. I didn't know how they related to music, but I saw what they were.

I was nervous on the day of the test but felt I actually did fairly well. The next week when the music teacher came into class, she said, "I am very pleased with a student." This student surprised her with how well all the questions were answered. When she called my name, I was stunned. I didn't move or look around. I had one thought. I remember it vividly; it played over and over in my mind. The small nine year old boy thought: "Maybe I'm not as stupid as everyone says I am."

The words Ms. Fenn spoke that day were the first positive words from a teacher I had received in three years. Those words changed my life. They gave me hope. I clung to those first thoughts that went through my mind: "Maybe I'm not as stupid as everyone says I am." It took years for me to make up what I hadn't learned in those early grades. More often than not, I took every book home at night and studied each of them diligently. My grades improved, although the wounds remained in my heart.

After high school, I began my formal martial arts training. The discipline helped my life but not my wounds. I wasn't very sociable due to a lack of friends and a low level of social skills. I trained in the martial arts faithfully. I gained respect from my peers, but I was still broken inside. I was a child inside and didn't want to be close to anyone who might laugh at me, make fun of me, or call me names. Coming to Christ and knowing I was accepted and loved by him initiated a long healing process.

Sometimes, when I did something unintentional and harmlessly humorous, people would laugh. They were responding to something innocent, but I would often respond with explosive rage in my words and actions. I had enough discipline to know how to avoid hurting others, but there were a number of emotional walls hindering my ability to make friends. Often my anger was directed back to myself, because I felt that there had to be something wrong with me. It wasn't easy when others would say, "You are no fun," or "What's the matter, can't you take a joke?" No, I couldn't. It wasn't funny; it was painful. Those wounds deep inside were being cut and reopened. There was a line that could be drawn, and it was crossed when the words and jokes were no longer humorous.

I put up the emotional walls to protect myself. It didn't take much for those wounds to be opened. I felt inferior, and I thought there was something wrong with me. I was wounded and didn't know how to overcome the feelings of rage and bitterness. I didn't know how to heal. It took years of people speaking good words and prophecies to me for the Lord to bring healing.

"Nor foolish talking nor testing which are not convenient but rather giving of thanks." (Ephesians 5:4)

Our jesting, joking and making fun of others always causes pain.

"Folly is joy to him who is destitute of wisdom." (Proverbs 15:21)

"Practical jokes" generally are aimed at the most vulnerable in a given group. Those who lack wisdom seem to derive some perverse pleasure in seeing someone else suffer pain, embarrassment, or even humiliation. This is the opposite of the Christian response. Christians are kind to the feebleminded. Christians give to the poor and lift up those who are down. Christians derive joy in seeing others helped, healed, or blessed. Tis is called "love." Those who have no wisdom and no understanding of God's perspective on life delight in just the opposite. They derive joy in seeing other people hurt or humiliated.

One day, a man in our church was joking about my favorite professional football team. He said, "Anyone who would root for this team has an elevator that doesn't go to the top floor." My facial expression in response to his taunts became a green light to keep pouring comments about me for several minutes. My wounds were feeling raw. He didn't know what his words were doing to me. He was a karate student of mine, a holder of a black belt. I kept my composure as best as I could. He stopped and looked at me as I just moved away.

He commented to someone that I looked as though I was going to rip his face off.

I knew that my non-verbal response was not the love of Christ coming through. Even pastors may have wounds. I did. Those wounds limited my effectiveness, and I was a spiritual zombie, alive but wounded. Again, it took words of encouragement, edification, and comfort from my brothers and sisters in Christ to salve those wounds and start a healing process in me.

This chapter has been the most difficult to write. I avoided rewriting and editing this chapter for weeks. I found excuses and other tasks, which I could do. I believe from my own experience and what I have seen in others that there are wounds from words, which need words to help heal. The wounds were started from words, and prophetic words were needed to bring healing. The Bible, especially Proverbs, teaches on the power of words. I cannot quote scriptures, which would prove exactly that word wounds need spiritual words or prophecies to aid in the healing process. It worked for me, and it has helped others.

The apostle Luke recorded the event in the temple when Jesus Christ quoted from Isaiah. The truths he proclaimed related to the power of words and the ministry we should emulate.

"The Spirit of the Lord is upon me because he has anointed me" (Luke 4:18; Isaiah 61:1).

• To preach the gospel to the poor.

• The gospel is good news. The gospel is good words to those who lack good words; they are life-changing words.

• He has sent me to heal the brokenhearted.

• He will heal and touch the innermost parts of our wounds and life.

• To proclaim liberty to the captive.

• He has the power to set us free from the bondage of words spoken over or to us.

• And recovery of sight to the blind.

• I was blind as to why I reacted in certain ways. It was the effect of words. When I saw and understood, the healing began.

• To set at liberty those who are oppressed.

• The wounds from words carry a weight and thought process that is a heavy yoke. He brings freedom.

• To proclaim the acceptable year of the Lord. Now is the acceptable year to be healed of word wounds.

Chapter 11

Wounded Warrior Healing

Words have amazing power to heal those who have been or are wounded by words. Victims of abuse, especially mental abuse, remain trapped in a relationship by the power of words. Actions may be unspoken words in motion. If we see body language like someone rolling their eyes upward as we are talking to them, the action tells us without saying a word that they do not believe what we are saying.

Actions that are negative are interpreted in our minds with our thoughts. Thoughts are words inside our minds. Ignoring someone who is talking to you is an action. You are saying by the action that the one speaking is not important, that you choose not to listen for some reason. Be careful about what you say with your actions.

"...that you study to be quiet...that you aspire to lead a quiet life." (1 Thessalonians 4:11)

Are we quiet? Do we try to lead a quiet life? Strife and disquiet enter lives when words that are better left unsaid are spoken. "I'll give them a piece of my mind." "I certainly told them off." "I don't understand why you want." Is it worth the strife and anxiety these words cause? I've noticed when people "fly off the handle" or "go nuts over something" It very seldom ends well. The words spoken are destructive to those hearing them.

Consider the words of Christ:

A good man out of the good treasure of his heart brings forth good; and an evil man out of the evil treasure of his heart brings forth evil. For out of the abundance of the heart, the mouth speaks. (Luke 6:45)

A good man out of the good treasure of his heart brings forth good things, and an evil man out of the evil treasure brings forth evil things. But I say to you that for every idle word men may speak, they will give account of it in the Day of Judgment. For by your words you will be justified and by your words you will be condemned. (Matthew 12:35–37)

Words Reveal Who You Are

The words, which we speak, are revelations. They reveal who we are and how we think. What comes out of our mouths in an angry outburst is as much a revelation of who we are as words of kindness. So we tend to say, "I didn't mean it. I was upset and angry." Only what is inside us can come out. How much we need to keep our hearts pure before the Lord!

Think On These Things

Be anxious for nothing, but in everything by prayer and supplication let your requests be made known to God; and the peace of God which surpasses all understanding will guard your hearts and minds through Christ Jesus. Finally, Brethren, whatever things are true, whatever things are noble, whatever things are just, whatever things are pure, whatever things are lovely, whatever things are of good report, if there is any virtue and if there is anything praise worthy–meditate on these things. (Philippians 4:6–8)

How we think will eventually find expression in our words. Don't let your mouth control who you are. The more we think or meditate on the good things God has done or who he is, the greater the chance of blessing and not curses (hurtful words, destructive speaking) will flow out of our mouths. When we are upset, we need to cool down, praise and thank the Lord, and not allow our words to control the situation or control us. Let rivers of living water, not anything hurtful, flow from your innermost being.

Prepare To Stand With Armor

The world in which we live would be much nicer if everyone spoke blessings. But not everyone is nice, and at certain times, words will come your way, which are not going to be blessings. What are we going to do? How will we prepare or be prepared for words, which try to harm us? One series of metaphors for spiritual preparation is to be put on the armor of God as stated in Ephesians 6:13–18:

• *Therefore, take up the whole armor of God that you may be able to withstand in the evil day and having done all to stand. Stand therefore having girded your waist with truth.* (verse 13).

This is the center of your body. It is where movement begins. The foundation for moving with God is the truth brought forth by his word, the Bible.

• *Having put on the breastplate of righteousness.* (verse 14)

• The righteousness is the righteousness of Christ which guards our heart.

• *And having your feet shod with the preparation of the gospel of peace.* (verse 15)

Everywhere we walk the gospel of peace should go. The word "gospel" means good news. We should speak good news and peace wherever we walk.

• *Above all, taking the shield of faith with which you will be able to quench all the fiery darts of the wicked one.* (verse 16)

"*A man who bears false witness against his neighbor is like a club, a sword and a sharp arrow*" (Proverbs 25:18). "*Their tongue is an arrow shot out; it speaks deceit*" (Jeremiah 3:8). "*Who wet their tongue like a sword, and bend their bows to shoot their arrows, even bitter words, that they may shoot in secret at the perfect: suddenly, do they shoot at him and fear not*" (Psalm 64:3–4). The knowledge of who you are in Christ; who and what God through his word says you are is a part of your faith. Faith comes by hearing and hearing by the word of God.

• *And take the helmet of salvation.* (Ephesians 6:17)

The helmet protects your mind. Your mind is the seat of your thoughts; so the helmet of salvation, of spiritual wholeness, protects your thought life.

• *And the sword of the spirit which is the word of God.* (verse 18)

This is the rhema or spoken word of God, sometimes referred to as the living word of God. It comes to us to be used as a sword by speaking the word of God.

We need to know who we are in Christ and the protection the armor has for us. We also need to pray in the spirit. Almost everyone has been wounded to some degree by words. Most of us have wounded others by our words. We cannot see the "word wounds" of others and may never know the depth of the wounds of the people, friends, and family in our life. We can pray for them, prophesy to them, and allow God to start a healing in their lives.

For us and for others, forgiveness is a key toward healing our wounds. I believe that words of forgiveness and blessing should be spoken out loud so that our words counter the words spoken to or about us. "I forgive those who have not spoken well of me." By not forgiving, we allow their words to remain as a coil of barbed wire in our spirits and our emotions. Forgiving allows us to be free from the bondage words create in our lives.

Prophecy, to speak with the Holy Spirit's inspiration to edify, exhort, and comfort, is a balm or salve for wounds. Prophecy touches the emotions and soul, but the real ministry happens in the human spirit. Christ took Peter, James, and John to be close to him in the garden of Gethsemane. Why did he do that? It was because their presence was a source of strength for him. Without saying a word, or even knowing what to say, their spirits ministered to him by their presence. I was recently watching the way people ministered by their presence at a funeral showing. Their presence and their words ministered on a spiritual level to comfort the bereaved. There is more action on a spiritual level than on the emotional level at a funeral. There is also interaction on a spiritual level when we offer fellowship. There is also a great supernatural interaction when we prophesy!

It is important to prophesy. It is vital to have a passion for prophesy. It is the life-changing, spiritual healing weapon of the body of Christ, which is rising from the dust of being forgotten, coming out of the closet of misunderstanding and bringing the glory of the throne room of God to be a river of living water to enlighten, bless, and encourage the church of the living God. For too long, prophecy has been ignored, forgotten, and relegated to the back room of insignificance. We, the individuals who are the body of Christ, will use prophecy to bring light into darkness and to move with the Holy Spirit in a river of living water. It is a key to healing wounded warriors and so much more.

Chapter 12

Prophecy Is Life Changing

In the tenth chapter of 1 Samuel, Saul the son of Kish is anointed to be King of Israel. Samuel then tells Saul what is going to happen when Saul goes home.

When you have departed from me today, you will find two men by Rachel's tomb in the territory of Benjamin at Zelzah; and they will say to you: "The donkeys which you went to look for have been found. And now your Father has ceased caring about the donkeys and is worrying about you saying, "What shall I do about my son?

Then you shall go forward from there and come to the Terebinth Tree of Tabor. There three men going up to God at Bethel will meet you, one carrying three young goats, another carrying three loaves of bread, and another carrying a skin of wine. And they will greet you and give you two loaves of bread, which you shall receive from their hands.

After that, you shall come to the hill of God where the Philistine Garrison is. And it will happen, when you have come there to the city; that you will meet a group of prophets coming down from the high place with a stringed instrument, a tambourine, a flute, and a harp before them, and they will be prophesying.

Then the Spirit of the Lord will come upon you and you will prophesy with them and be turned into another man. And let it be, when these signs come to you, that you do as the occasion demands; for God is with you. You shall go down before me to Gilgal; and surely I will come down to you to offer burnt offerings and make sacrifices of peace offerings. Seven days you shall wait till I come to you and show you what you should do.

So it was, when he had turned his back to go from Samuel that God gave him another heart; and all those signs came to pass that day. When they came there to the hill, there was a group of prophets to meet him; then the Spirit of God came upon him, and he prophesied among them. And it happened, when all who knew him formerly saw that he indeed prophesied among the prophets; that the people said to one another; "What is this that has come upon the son of Kish? Is Saul also among the prophets?"

Then a man from there answered and said; "But, who is the Father?" Therefore it became a Proverb: "Is Saul also among the prophets?" And when he had finished prophesying, he went to the high place. (1 Samuel 10:2–12)

Saul was turned into another man. God gave him another heart. Verse six states: *"The Spirit of the Lord will come upon you and you **will prophesy** with them and be turned into another man."* Now, God in his omnipotence could have turned Saul into another man with another heart without having him prophesy, but he chose to have him prophesy.

This must have continued to become a proverb: *"Is Saul also among the prophets?"* Prophecy brings the heart of God to the people. It changes you as you become a vessel of living water. There is a choice in what we do. Verse seven reminds us: *"And let it be that you do as the occasion demands; for God is with you."* We should choose to let it be; we are to allow God to move in and through us as the occasion demands. Prophecy will bring changes in our lives as we learn to be more sensitive to the Holy Spirit and more attuned to the heart of God.

Later, Saul was trying to kill David. King Saul was told that David was at Naioth in Ramah.

Then Saul sent messengers to take David. And when they saw the group of prophets prophesying, and Samuel standing as leader over them, the Spirit of God came upon the messengers of Saul and they also prophesied. And when Saul was told, he sent other messengers, and they prophesied likewise. Then Saul sent messengers again for the third time, and they prophesied also. Then he also went to Ramah, and came to the great well that is at Sechu. So he asked, and said, "Where are Samuel and David?" And someone said, "Indeed they are at Naioth in Ramah." So he went to Naioth in Ramah. Then, the Spirit of God was upon him also, and he went on and prophesied until he came to Naioth in Ramah. And he also stripped off his clothes and prophesied before Samuel in like manner, and lay down naked all that day and all that night. Therefore they say; "Is Saul also among the prophets?" (1 Samuel 19:20–24)

Saul's messengers were unable to kill or capture David. When Saul went after David he was prevented from doing what he wished to do by the Spirit of the Lord and by prophesying. Saul was turned into another man. The Lord gave him a new heart. I believe that when we earnestly seek to prophesy and are willing to practice, the heart of our Lord is revealed to us through our own words. When we hear how the Lord speaks through us, through prophecy, and by the power of the Holy Spirit, our heart will also be changed as living water flows from us to give life to others. Prophecy is a manifestation of the love of our Father and the Lord Jesus Christ through the words we speak.

Prophecy Gives Life

Not only is prophecy life-changing, but it gives life. Prophecy imparts spiritual life to us. Consider the passage in Ezekiel 37. Ezekiel was taken by the spirit in the midst of the valley of dry bones. He prophesied to them and the bones came together and were covered with sinews and flesh. Then, he prophesied for breath:

So I prophesied as he commanded and breath came into them, and they lived, and stood upon their feet, an exceedingly great army. Then he said to me; "Son of man, these bones are the whole house of Israel, they indeed say, our bones are dry, our hope is lost, and we ourselves are cut off! Therefore, prophesy and say to them, 'thus says the Lord God: Behold, O my people, I will open your graves and cause you to come up from your graves and bring you into the land of Israel. Then you shall know that I am the Lord when I have opened your graves O my people, and brought you up from your graves. I will put my Spirit in you, and you shall live; and I will place you in your own land. Then you shall know that I, the Lord, have spoken it and performed it, says the Lord. (Ezekiel 37:10–14)

We sometimes view the Old Testament prophets as being doom and gloom prognosticators. When God's judgment was imminent and national defeat was coming, they brought forth that message. They also brought life, hope, and encouragement to the people. That is what New Testament prophecy does. It brings spiritual life to those who receive prophecy.

One of the most powerful prophesies I have received was during a trying time of growth. A close brother said, "It is going to be okay." Six words, simply stated, but they were so very strong. Before he finished speaking, I felt as though two gigantic hands had reached inside of me and grabbed my spirit and squeezed it, not to a point of discomfort, but very tightly. The Holy Spirit whispered, "I have you, and I am holding you. I will walk with you. I will hold you this tight so nothing will happen to you. It is going to be okay." Those words were life to my dry bones.

Prophecy Brings the Word to Life

The Word of God, the Bible, is the written word, the logos. Prophecy takes the logos and brings rhema, the spoken lifegiving word. "It is going to be all right." In my spirit, those words confirmed that *"he will never leave us and never forsake us"* (Hebrews 13:5). Even though in this instance the prophecy was not an exact quote from the scriptures, it brought life to that passage.

Prophecy will never go against the Word of God, but will confirm and bring life to the written Word. Prophecy is sometimes the very Word of God, the Bible, spoken under the anointing to bring life to dry bones. We, in our humanity, may never know how dry someone's spiritual bones are or how spiritually dead they may feel, but a word of prophecy may renew and give spiritual life unto them.

Prophecy is a powerful gift of blessing to the body of Christ. Are we willing to follow Paul's admonitions and earnestly desire to prophesy? Are we going to become life-giving, life-changing rivers of living water to those around us?

Chapter 13

Prophecy is a Light into the Darkness

Your word is a lamp to my feet and a light to my path (Psalm 119:105).

In him was life, and the life was the light of men (John 1:9).

That was the true light which gives light to every man coming into the world (John 1:9).

You are the light of the world. A city that is set on a hill cannot be hidden. Nor do they light a lamp and put it under a basket, but on a lampstand, and it gives light to all who are in the house. Let your light so shine before men, that they may see your good works and glorify your Father in heaven (Matthew 5:14–16).

His Word is Light

In Psalm 119, the main idea is that the Word of God, the Holy Bible, gives us light or understanding as we travel through this life. John tells us that Christ's life is the light of men and he gives light to every man. We also are to be the light of the world so that others may see what we do and how we speak.

In the thirty-fourth chapter of Exodus, Moses came down from Mount Sinai. The skin of his face shone while he talked with God. When the children of Israel saw the shining countenance of Moses, he had to put a veil on until he went in to talk with God again. Now Moses was over eighty years old. He had spent the previous forty years as a shepherd out in the wind and sun. I imagine he had a craggy, weather-beaten face full of wrinkles, but in the presence of God, his face radiated the glory of God.

When Jesus met with Moses and Elijah on the Mount of Transfiguration, "*his face shone like the sun, and his clothes became as white as the light*" (Matthew 17:2). When he was exiled on the prison island of Patmos, the apostle John saw the New Jerusalem illuminated by the glory of God. "*The Lamb is its light*" (Revelation 21:23).

God is light; the Lamb is light. Moses was in the presence of God, and his face shone. Jesus was transfigured, and he shone like the sun. I have heard comments to expectant mothers indicating they had a glow about them. Could this be because another life with its light is growing inside her womb?

For you were once darkness but now you are light in the Lord. Walk as children of light (Ephesians 5:8).

How is it that we walk as children of light? Paul contrasts sin as darkness and righteousness as light. We are to expose the unfruitful works of darkness. Then, in verse thirteen, he says *"All things that are exposed are made manifest by the light, for whatever makes manifest is light."* Sometimes, our lifestyles bring light. Sometimes, our words bring light.

If we are to let our light shine, we must let our manner of life and our words be light. We are to speak to one another in psalms and hymns and spiritual songs, *"giving thanks always for all things to God the Father in the name of our Lord Jesus Christ"* (Ephesians 5:20).

Paul talks of the unfruitful works of darkness in Ephesians chapter 5 and verse 11. Darkness portrays not only sin but a spiritual state. Sinners are in darkness not only as a lifestyle but as a spiritual state. They cannot see God's grace and goodness until the light of the gospel enters their world. Paul stated, *"That by the foolishness of preaching (sharing the gospel), men would be saved. The gospel is light. It is preached (spoken); those words are light."*

Spiritual Words are Light

If preaching the gospel is done with words and those words are light and bring light into a darkened spiritual state, how many of our spoken words are light? The gospel is. I believe prayers are light; prophecy is light; teaching brings light and understanding. What if we realized that praying, preaching, prophesying, and singing spiritual songs were actually beams of light shining into the spiritual darkness?

Would that change our understanding of why it is necessary to pray, sing, and give thanks? They are lights shining into a spiritually dark world. Therefore, every time we pray, prophesy, share Jesus, and sing or give thanks, it is penetrating the darkness of the world around us. When we join together with others there is more light generated. The closer we move to the Lord, the greater our light and our words become.

Prayers are Light
Imagine the millions of shafts of light that quit shining when prayer was removed from our public schools. Every day during the school year, there was light from prayer. I am old enough to remember praying before lunch. We could not eat until everyone was back in the classroom and we prayed. We walked through a line, picked up our tray and milk, and went back to our classrooms to eat at our desks after prayer. Without those millions of shafts of light, how dark have our schools become?

Do we see what is going on in our communities? If we just observe without praying, it is like walking into a dark room and noticing darkness and then walking out. If you turn on the light switch there is light. Prayer is the light switch for our world. Every time we pray, there is light. It may be just a little candle, but it is light. It is important and it does make a difference. Our problem is that because it is spiritual light shining in spiritual darkness, we cannot see what is going on with our natural eyes. When we flip a light switch and light illuminates the room, we can see. When we pray, the light goes into the spiritual darkness, and it makes a difference.

Thanksgiving is Light
When we give thanks, it is a light in the darkness. It may be a night light; something to help us not stub our toes on what we would otherwise not be aware of. Give thanks for all things; there are to be no exceptions or no exemptions, and nothing gets a pass. When we give thanks, we have night lights to help us. When we complain, we shut off the night lights and have to grope blindly in our misunderstanding. I am writing, not about thanking God for our food or our great blessings, but for what seems impossible to understand. Giving thanks for what breaks our heart and turns our world upside down, inside out, and topsy-turvy. Those are the times when our path is so dark that our understanding is so limited and our tears blur our vision so much that without the night lights of thanksgiving, we stumble around, feeling lost.

It is also a command in the New Testament to give thanks. I have heard people say how spiritual Paul and Silas were when they were beaten and jailed at Philippi, and they were praying, giving thanks, and singing. I think they were too physically uncomfortable to sleep and too hurt and miserable to do anything else but to cry out to God. Those are the times when we need a night light.

Sermons and Teachings are Light

Every Sunday, there is light shining into the spiritual darkness from Sunday school classes and the pulpits of Churches. There is light from our words and the word of God. It happens not only on Sunday mornings but during the whole week. There is light from every home, church, fellowship gathering (not social gathering), and every prayer meeting.

Each time someone is absent, there is a little less light. You are important; your presence is important. It is lending a spiritual presence not only to the Lord but also to his body. It adds light to shine in the darkness. When you share something from a sermon or teaching, you are sending light into darkness.

When you share the word of God, it not only is light but a two-edged sword to cut the authority of the darkness. Do you understand the concept of being light to a lost world? Considering my words, your words, my prayers, and your prayers as actual rays of light shining in the darkness helps me to see how important it is by doing what we do. It is light.

Prophecy is Light

When the Holy Spirit authors our words through his unction and anointing, the brightness is magnified. I look at prophecy as the street lights on our path. Traveling down an interstate, it is great to see the lights of a rest area or the outskirts of a town by those lights. Prophecy should be to edify, exhort, and comfort. It should be the street light of our journey of life. It helps, and it may allow some things to be seen by its light, which we might miss without that light or understanding. Should we not desire to have our life's interstate lit? Should we not desire to do what we can to help someone else down their road?

I was recently asked, "What is prophecy?" Prophecy is Holy Spirit anointed speaking to edify, exhort, and comfort.

"The testimony of Jesus is the spirit of prophecy"(Revelation 19:10).

What is it? It is speaking by inspiration to glorify the Lord, to edify, build up the hearers, to exhort, and to comfort. That is what it does. It edifies, exhorts, and comforts. Prophecy builds up, stirs up, and lifts up. **Prophecy is a manifestation of God's love to someone through our words given by the Holy Spirit.**

Someone once said to me, "I was hesitant to speak a word to someone because I didn't want to be wrong."

I replied that I was the opposite. I am willing to be wrong trying to bring a manifestation of our Father's love into someone's life. I do not want to miss the opportunity to bring the Father's love from his throne into someone's life. That is a great privilege. The apostle Paul advised us *"to desire earnestly to prophecy."* It is light to shine into someone's life. It is a river of living water.

Chapter 14

Prophecy is a Current in Our River

These last chapters have resulted from months of seeking the Lord for wisdom and understanding. I have written in previous chapters that Paul, in 1 Corinthians, emphasized the spiritual gifts, especially prophecy. Why was there such an emphasis on prophecy, and why is it largely ignored by the body of Christ? Even Pentecostal and Charismatic assemblies seem to miss the mark in this area. Why? What knowledge or understanding of this gift and its use has dwindled and almost disappeared from the fellowship of believers? What is its purpose? How is it to be used? What are the benefits?

My spirit has been stirred to seek for the understanding of why Paul emphasized this gift. I pray that the eyes of our understanding will be opened to the immense value of this gift and the body of Christ will know why "*all may prophesy.*" I have a deep sense and leading of the Holy Spirit, which has guided me to a greater knowledge that burns within me. To know prophecy may be life changing. To understand it brings healing to wounded warriors. To be illuminated to the light of prophecy, we should stir in us that earnest desire to prophesy. To all those, I am adding this chapter. I believe prophecy is a current of the spiritual river of life. If you are in a canoe going downstream in a river, the current moves you along.

 "*For prophecy never came by the will of man, but Holy men of God spoke as they were moved by the Holy Spirit*" (2 Peter 1:21).

The idea is of a ship carried by the current or a sailing vessel using the wind to make its progress. Prophecy is that current in our lives. It doesn't choose our course. It doesn't make us do something. It is the undercurrent in our spiritual life to help us on our journey. It is a powerful dynamic force for our good. Wow!

"*But Mary kept all these things and powered them in her heart*" (Luke 2:19).

"*Then he went down with them and came to Nazareth and was subject to them, but his mother kept all these things in her heart*" (Luke 2:51).

Verse nineteen was in response to the shepherds coming to see the baby Jesus and bringing the words the angels spoke to them: *"Do not be afraid, for behold, I bring you tidings of great joy which will be to all people. For there is born to you this day in the city of David, a Savior, who is Christ the Lord."* Mary kept these words and added them to the words of Gabriel and Elizabeth. They were a current in her life.

Verse fifty-one was after the feast of the Passover at Jerusalem. Jesus, who was twelve years old at the time, was accidentally left behind. When Joseph and Mary returned to look for him, they found him in the temple, sitting in the midst of the teachers. He was listening, asking questions, and astonishing them with his answers. Jesus said to Mary and Joseph, *"Why did you seek me? Do you not know that I must be about my Father's business?"* The words of Christ were a prophecy she kept in her heart and which became a current to help her through the emotional trauma of the crucifixion of her son, of God's Son. I believe those words continued their flow past the Passover sacrifice to the resurrection, the upper room, and the ministry she had in the early church.

Prophecy Aids in Warfare
"Tis charge I commit to you, son Timothy, according to the prophecies previously made concerning you, that by them you may wage the good warfare" (1 Timothy 1:18).

We do not know what was prophesied to Timothy, but we know they involved strong words of affirmation, exhortation, and blessing. God knew all about the spiritual battles and persecution Timothy would face, and the prophetic team not only conveyed the words from the Lord he would need but also supernatural grace. With just this understanding, I want to cry out to the Lord and my brothers and sisters and say, "Help us to prophesy and impart this supernatural grace and wisdom other believers need to fight their spiritual battles."

Prophecy Manifests Gifts
"Do not neglect the gift that is in you which was given to you by prophecy with the laying on of the hands of the eldership" (1 Timothy 4:14).

Paul believed this gift was important to Timothy. He reminded Timothy in the next verse to meditate; that is, to memorize, visualize, and personalize the prophecies that were given to him by the *presbuteros*, the senior Christian leaders. *"Give yourself entirely to them that your progress may be evident to all."* I believe Paul introduced a spiritual principle here. All prophecies are good, but when we meditate on them, when we give ourselves to them, when we yield to the power of the prophecy, their effect in our lives will be proportional to our obedience and our faith. I know there are those who keep a prophetic journal of what was spoken to them so that those truths from God are not forgotten or neglected in their lives. How much of the current of our spiritual river is lost because we so lightly esteem what is spoken to us through prophecy?

Prophecy Continues With Us

"Therefore, I remind you to stir up the gift (charisma) *of God which is in you through the laying on of my hands. For God has not given us a spirit of fear, but of power* (Dunamis— supernatural miracle—working power) *and of love and of a sound mind"* (2 Timothy 1).

The context suggests that the gift given was to aid Timothy, but he had the responsibility of stirring it up. God has given us, not a fearful spirit, but a powerful, loving spirit, which does not fight against our intelligence, our good judgment, our understanding, or our ability to make good decisions. Here is another area of battle. To know our spiritual life is going to be a walk of faith, believing what we can't see or totally understand and what we do know and understand.

The effect or the power of prophecy is subject to our willingness to stir it up, to yield to it, and to honor the words with our understanding and action. When we do, the power continues to be a current in our spiritual life. Knowing this, is your spirit being stirred to allow prophecy to gain its proper place in your life? Do you have the desire Paul tells us to have? Do your words and your prophecies have the river of living water flowing from your innermost being? Lord, grant us the grace and desire to prophesy. Let us be instruments of blessing as we yield our heart and tongue to the gracious promptings of the Holy Spirit.

As every man hath received the gift, even so minister the same one to another, as good stewards of the manifold grace of God. If any man speaks, let him speak as the oracles of God; if any man ministers, let him do it as of the ability which God giveth. (1 Peter 4:10–11)

Chapter 15

Learn To Be Sensitive

For as many as are led by the spirit of God, these are sons of God. (Romans 8:14)

We as Christians should constantly strive to be sensitive to the leading of the Holy Spirit. The cares and business of our days tend to cause us to focus on the tasks at hand, or the planning of the next steps of our day. These preoccupations may make us insensitive to the gentle nudges of the Holy Spirit. At times we may dismiss those spiritual tugs altogether.

Recently, I stopped by Culligan, our local bottled water distributor to pick up a five-gallon jug of water and return an empty container. As I was finishing the last few drops of my morning coffee before I getting out of my car, a sport utility vehicle pulled in beside me, and a young woman exited. She opened the back door to grab a child from the car seat and then went to the rear of the vehicle. I had to go to the side of my car where they were to pick up my empty water container. A boy was climbing down from the seat, and he and I smiled and waved at each other. When I placed the full container of water in my back seat, he was carrying two one gallon containers to be filled. I mentioned that he was a big help carrying those jugs. I noticed the way the mother interacted with her child. She brought a chair over for the boy to stand on and push the button to dispense the water. I finished paying and drove away.

As I was driving, I thought about not only how I saw the mother interacting with her son but also what I felt about two miles down the road. I was feeling prompted by the Spirit to say something to that mother. My first thought was that it was probably just me thinking those thoughts. After the second nudge, I thought she had probably already left. When the third leading came, I looked at the time to see how much time I had left to do everything I had planned. I started to calculate how much time I would lose by turning around but realized that the Holy Spirit was leading and going back to speak to her was the top priority at that time.

She was filling her last jug when I walked back into Culligan's. One of the workers asked how he could help, and I said, "Everything was taken care of for me. I just came back to say something to this young woman." He went around the corner and stopped to listen to what I had to say. I complimented her on the interaction with her son. I don't remember exactly what I said to her. I do remember her hand coming up and covering her mouth (as if she was shocked). She then thanked me and said that my remarks had made her day.

It would have been easy to ignore or dismiss that nudging or leading to go back and speak to the young mother, but I try to practice what I preach or write. It is not always an easy thing to be sensitive and be led by the Holy Spirit. It almost always involves choices and decisions and sacrifices. It is a blend of our human will and divine leading. Much of the time we may never see or comprehend the results of our sensitivity and obedience to those leadings. What is important is that we learn to be sensitive and obedient. If I would have thought much longer about going back, she would have left and the opportunity also would have left with her.

How Do You Know What To Say?
I am frequently asked, "How do you know what to say?" Many times I am at a total loss for words. I have an urge or leading to say something, but no words emerge to go with the leading. Other times, I may have three or four words or an opening sentence. I would not have the urge or leading if the Holy Spirit was not going to continue leading and help me find the right words to say. I have learned I can trust and rely on the Holy Spirit, but I have to be willing to start.

I have found a few sentences, which help me start when I am unsure of what to say. One is "I feel God's hands on your life and." (Hopefully, the Holy Spirit helps at this juncture). Another sentence is "I appreciate the way you" or "I want to thank you for being (doing, etc.)." There is no memorized formula. If there were one, I would probably try to copyright it and make it available to everyone. It is a blending of our will and our choices with the guidance of the Holy Spirit. It isn't hard, but it's not always easy either. All we need to do is open our mouths and surrender our minds to the leading of the Holy Spirit. It isn't easy to get our doubts, fears, and uncertainties out of the way of our simple obedience. The more we desire to prophesy and are willing to be obedient, the more our faith grows with our ability.

What If I'm Wrong or Make a Mistake?

I appreciate the concern we should all have about staying sensitive in our spirit to the Holy Spirit so that we may prophesy correctly. We are human. We will never do everything perfectly. It will always be a blending of the divine guidance of the Holy Spirit and our imperfect souls and spirits. If you make a mistake or have an imperfect delivery, will the earth stop rotating? Suppose you look in the mirror and no longer recognize your image? These are extreme examples, but the answer is still "no." A mistake is just an opportunity to learn and improve. Remember that in the kingdom of God motive is vitally important. If you are motivated by love rather than a desire to be important or get rich, you will be blessed in reaching out with an inspired word. God looks into the heart.

I almost always state: "I would rather be wrong trying to edify, exhort, and comfort than to miss the opportunity for God to love someone through the words I speak." How are we going to err? If I am speaking to bless another person and it isn't led and anointed by the Holy Spirit, it will just be good words. It is going to be good. The Scripture tells us to watch our words, speak truth, and exhort one another. The words will be good even if we do not do everything perfectly. I do not want to miss the opportunity to bring a blessing into someone's life.

Guidelines For Sensitivity

Prophecy is to edify, exhort, and comfort. Put another way; our speaking God's words to others will build them up spiritually. It will draw them to the Lord and give them direction and encouragement and will bring peace or rest to their spirits. True prophecies are not usually directives such as "You need to forgive." The person may have an issue with forgiveness, so it might be stated like this; "I feel (or sense, or discern) that the Lord would have you pray and see if there is anything or anybody you have not forgiven, which might be limiting the Lord's grace in your life."

We want to be cautious that we are not telling someone what or how to live their lives, because we are commanded to refrain from *lording over people* (1 Peter 5:3).

Someone once told me, "You wanted to do something and had thought, I want to do this." The exact nature of the impulse was not really important, but I was being told what I wanted and how I thought. It wasn't true. However, I did pray about it and sought the Lord and said, "If this is what you want me to do, I am open and willing." Even though the delivery was wrong, there was still an element of truth to be extracted from the prophecy. I am learning to "eat the fish and spit out the bones."

All prophecy must have a basis of love. It should flow from and be enriched with God's love. I received another prophecy which was given gently, encased with God's love, which spoke to me as truth. I was being told that the trial was not over, that there would be more pain to come, but the hand of the Lord would be on me and fruit would abound when it was over. I wasn't overjoyed at being told there was more pain and the trial wasn't over, but at the same time, I received a comforting peace and assurance from the prophecy. I also sensed an overwhelming sense of love as it was being spoken.

We Do Not Have to Accept Prophecy

We do not have to accept prophecy that is against the word of God or words we are not comfortable with. People do make mistakes. Sometimes, the intent or desire is real, but what happens is that personal thoughts or ideas take precedent over what the Spirit is really saying. It has happened only a few times to me.

Recently, a sincere believer said to me: "You could be one of the great theologians of our time, but you must go through more pain and you must come clean." First, I am not called to be a theologian (whether great or not so great!). Secondly, to say I must or have to go through more pain is a directive, which goes against the nature or essence of prophecy. Third, the command to "come clean" implied that I must have had hidden sin in my life. We all have sin, but with daily confession, forgiving others, and asking for forgiveness, why should I need to come clean? I prayed over this. It was a battle. The words seemed to bring a heaviness and oppression to my spirit. That was not from the Holy Spirit.

Compare this to the prophecy mentioned before. Both stated there would be pain or trials, but one brought peace while the other brought a heaviness I had to fight against. We are responsible for how we react to or act upon prophecy. I have good prophecies written on cards that I keep on my desk to reread and draw strength and encouragement from.

Learning to be sensitive to the leading of the Holy Spirit and being willing to speak is a part of the process of fulfilling Paul's teaching on prophecy. We should also be sensitive to how our spirit reacts to prophecy or what is given as prophecy but may not be in line with biblical prophecy. My experience has been blessed by prophecies. There have been only a few, which I had to discern whether or not they were right. Most have edified, encouraged, and comforted, which have made my spiritual journey richer. To minister to one another with prophecy is a great blessing. It is a powerful tool of encouragement and only eternity will reveal the depth of impact prophecy has in our lives.

I believe what Paul wrote. *"We should earnestly desire; we should have a passion to prophesy."* I was enjoying Christian fellowship at a couple's home one Sunday when their neighbor stopped in for a visit. I spoke to her and felt a stirring in her spirit. I watched as tears came to her eyes, and she said, "I needed that. It is exactly what the Lord has been showing me."

I never want to miss the opportunity to allow God's love to touch someone's life through or by the words of prophecy I speak. I truly believe that prophecy is living water flowing from our innermost being.

Chapter 16

Rivers of Living Water

On the last day, that great day of the feast, Jesus stood and cried out saying; "If anyone thirsts, let him come to me and drink. He who believes in me, as the scripture has said, out of his heart will Flow Rivers of living water." But this he spoke concerning the spirit; "whom those believing in him would receive"; for the Holy Spirit was not yet given because Jesus was not yet glorified. (John 7:37–39)

Verse thirty-nine makes it clear that Jesus was saying "the Holy Spirit would make it possible for rivers of living water to flow from his heart or spirit." The preceding verses tell us that we must thirst for Jesus. We must desire to be close to Jesus, to know his heart. I have worked in the excavating field all of my life. Sometimes, the heat and work makes me thirsty. Many times I have consumed two quart bottles of Gatorade on my drive home. Do we have that same type of thirst for Jesus where we have to draw close to him?

What is living water? That which is alive, that which has the power to give life. It is spiritual and gives or imparts spiritual life to others. When Jesus was speaking to the Samaritan woman at Jacob's well (John 4), he prophesied to her that he could give her living water. How much did her life change after he spoke to her? She became an evangelist and brought the town to Jesus. He stayed two days and many believed in him. That had to be one of the longest church services. It lasted two days, and he spoke living water from the Holy Spirit.

How is the Holy Spirit going to move in us so that we can have rivers of living water flowing from our heart? If we follow the example of Christ, it will be with the words the Holy Spirit gives to us. Rivers of living water are not our ordinary daily talking but Spirit inspired words of prophecy. They should flow as a river to edify, exhort, and comfort.

From writing, I have gained a new understanding of why Paul was adamant about our pursuit of the prophetic. Why should we have a burning desire, a thirst, and a passion to prophesy? I have taught others about prophecy, and it is such an honor to see their growth, to see rivers of living water flow from them and bless the lives of others.

Jesus said that there would be rivers of living water flowing from our being. It is not to be a trickle of water. It is not to be a small stream or gentle brook. It is to be rivers of living water. Prophecy is a river of living water. Because rivers are plural, I believe prophecy is the only one of the rivers to flow from us. Sharing what Christ has done and who he is may be a river. Worship may be a river, but prophecy is a river of living water.

Words Have Power

Our words have power. They have life or destruction. We should know that our speech should be with grace and salt. James stated, "The tongue is an unruly evil and only Christ and the Holy Spirit will make our speech what it should be." It will be life-giving.

Blessing and Cursing/Complaining

How very important is our speech? How greatly does it affect our life? I pray the words, which are written will stir your hearts. Gaining a greater understanding of how we speak will lead us to yield our tongue to the Lord and to the Holy Spirit, and thereby to become an instrument of blessing.

Thanksgiving

Thanksgiving is a yielding of ourselves, our speech, and our thoughts to the divine providence of our Lord. Thanks and thanksgiving occurs over seventy times in the New Testament. In everything give thanks. That is a command, which brings blessings.

Desire To Prophesy

I sensed that in this writing there should first be an emphasis on understanding our words. The body of Christ and also those with whom we interact would be greatly blessed if we yielded our tongue to the Lord. Learning to yield to the Holy Spirit and to earnestly desire to prophesy will enable us to be a constant blessing to others. Will you allow this river of living water to flow from you? I believe prophecy is the most neglected and powerful aspect of blessing available to the body of Christ. I pray that this writing will help to bring light and understanding to you so that rivers of living water can flow.

Prophecy Is a Command
Follow after charity, and desire spiritual gifts, but rather that ye may prophesy. For he that speaketh in an unknown tongue speaketh not unto men, but unto God: for no man understandeth him; howbeit in the spirit he speaketh mysteries. But he that prophesieth speaketh unto men to edification, and exhortation, and comfort. (1 Corinthians 14:1–3)

Prophecy is possible
"For ye may all prophesy one by one, that all may learn, and all may be comforted" (1 Corinthians 14:31).

Prophecy is life-changing
And Ananias went his way, and entered into the house. and putting his hands on him said, Brother Saul, the Lord, even Jesus, that appeared unto thee in the way as thou camest, hath sent me, that thou mightest receive thy sight, and be filled with the Holy Ghost. And immediately there fell from his eyes as it had been scales: and he received sight forthwith, and arose, and was baptized. (Acts 9:17-18)

Prophecy is life-giving
Thus saith the Lord God; "Behold, O my people, I will open your graves, and cause you to come up out of your graves, and bring you into the land of Israel. And ye shall know that I am the Lord, when I have opened your graves, O my people and brought you up out of your graves. And shall put my spirit in you and ye shall live, and I shall place you in your own land: then shall ye know that I the Lord have spoken it, and performed it." (Ezekiel 37:12–14)

Prophecy is healing, a salve for wounds
And these signs shall follow them that believe; in my name shall they cast out devils; they shall speak with new tongues; they shall take up serpents; and if they drink any deadly thing, it shall not hurt them; they shall lay hands on the sick, and they shall recover. (Mark 16:17–18)

Prophecy is an expression of spiritual light. Walk in the light
God, who commanded the light to shine out of darkness, hath shined in our hearts, to give the light of the knowledge of the glory of God in the face of Jesus Christ.7 But we have this treasure in earthen vessels,

that the excellence of the power may be of God, and not of us. (2 Corinthians 4:6–7)

Prophecy is a current

"Neglect not the gift that is in thee, which was given thee by prophecy, with the laying on of the hands of the presbytery" (1 Timothy 4:14).

"Wherefore I put thee in remembrance that thou stir up the gift of God, which is in thee by the putting on of my hands. For God hath not given us the spirit of fear; but of power, and of love, and of a sound mind" (2 Timothy 1:6–7).

Prophecy is a manifestation of God's love. Let your gift of prophecy be an expression of his love to someone today.

But he that prophesieth speaketh unto men to edification, and exhortation, and comfort. He that speaketh in an unknown tongue edifieth himself; but he that prophesieth edifeth the church. I would that ye all spake with tongues, but rather that ye prophesied: for greater is he that prophesieth than he that speaketh with tongues, except he interpret, that the church may receive edifying. (1 Corinthians 14:3–5)

Testimonies

Brian's Testimony

I had asked God to take over my life because I needed change. I had lost sight of what life was all about three years previously. Three days later, I went to Jan's church and met a woman and her child. I had never met this woman before coming to church that day.

I had been praying to God about my life and asking for his help, but I only knew what that conversation was about. This is important to remember. We sang some songs. Jan talked some, and then he said that the Bible talks about edifying people or doing and saying something nice to people. Then he said, "Today, we are going to do that for Brian."

He asked the woman whom I had never met to start. She was not sure what to say to me. She smiled, looked at Jan and me for a few seconds and then stopped and looked at the floor. The smile left and she looked at me and proceeded to talk to me about the things I had talked to God about. She could not have known those things or the words I had used. I broke down and cried profusely.

Crystal's Testimony

My family and I have had many blessing from God. I feel God wants me to share what he has done for me at this point of my life. I want to share all my blessings and experiences, but that would be a book, so for now this is my testimony.

I want to share God's never-ending love, His many blessings and his mercy. I will start by saying that at the age of sixteen I denied Christ. I questioned whether God is real.

It was Thanksgiving morning in 2005. The day was cold and the roads were slushy. My sister-in-law and I had our four children with us. We were traveling down State road 5 toward Larwill. The intersection where we needed to turn had a slight incline. She was turning left and turned in front of an SUV. The truck hit the front passenger side where I was sitting. At that time, I didn't remember much of what happened. I was in and out of consciousness. When I was able to open my eyes, it was like looking at photographs through green fog.

I was screaming for help on the inside. Once I opened my eyes and saw my daughter sitting beside me. She had blood mixed with tears on her face of fear. I couldn't move to help her. I couldn't hear the three babies in the back seat. I remember feeling helpless because I was trapped and couldn't help my kids.

I was freezing, and it felt like hours had gone by before the EMS vehicle arrived. Later, I heard that they had asked someone if I had died. The next thing I remember was a medic holding my head and telling me it was all right, and they were going to get me out. He told me it was going to be loud because they had to use the "jaws of life" to cut me out. I don't remember anything until after they placed me in the ambulance.

I still had no idea what happened to my children. They kept asking me questions about who I was, who my kids were, and who they needed to call. I just wanted to know if my children were alive. My mind was overloaded with fear, questions, and thoughts of what if I didn't realize what kind of pain I was really in. Soon they placed my daughter in the ambulance with me. I was so scared, but I knew she was more frightened than I was. I remember her crying and saying "Mommy, Mommy," as they worked on her. "Mommy, are you okay?" she asked. It felt so good to hear her voice. I said, "Don't be scared. Let them do what they need. Jesus is here to help us. It's okay, baby."

We finally arrived at the hospital. My family was there waiting for us, but my husband was out of town working. I finally found out that my son, niece, and nephew were unhurt. Then, the news for my daughter and me came. They said she had stomach pains and a fractured eye. She needed to be sent to Fort Wayne. They sent her out and then told me it was my eye that was badly fractured. My cheek was crushed, and my hand and collarbone were broken. They put two plates and about fourteen screws in my face to repair the damage. The injuries later caused TMJ in my jaw. I have had problems with my ears since then. Several years later, different doctors and specialists had difficulty diagnosing the severe pains in my arms and legs. The pain caused muscle spasms and tingling. I couldn't walk three steps without falling. I lived in a reclining chair for a long time. I came to the point of asking God to take me home. I also remember telling my husband to shoot me to get this all over with.

At the time of the accident, I was not serving God. I grew up in church and knew in my heart that he was there, but I had fallen away. I believe God used this accident to reach me and pull me back to himself. I praise him that I was the only one with such trauma. Not one child had a severe injury. God blessed me with the injuries. He gave me the grace to avoid blaming my sister for this. Even during the hardest parts when I couldn't walk, I didn't blame her.

About two and a half years ago, God answered my prayer by sending a chiropractor my way. He took x-rays from my head to my toes and found severe whiplash in eight vertebrae in my back. Here is another blessing. The doctor said it had happened so long before that he didn't know how much he could help. He said it was possible that I would be like that for the rest of my life. It took three weeks of adjustments every other day. I was finally able to walk and put on my shoes. It was a miracle. I wouldn't be walking if not for that treatment. I still had the pain, weakness, tingling, and muscle spasms, but I was walking.

I struggled with that for two years. Ten October 7, 2011 came. My husband and I started attending a Bible study with a pastor in Columbia City. That night I was really hurting and just not feeling well. I had been at my wit's end for some time and just wanted it all to go away. The pastor had my brother and sister in Christ, and my husband pray over me and anoint me with oil. During this time, my nerves tingled, and I felt as if I was floating. After my husband was done, I felt hands holding me at my waist as the pain melted out of me. Today I have no pain whatsoever. I feel like a teenager again. God has done it. I now can be a wife, mother, and servant for Christ. You may share this with whomever you like.

Matt's Testimony

We can see a change in a person's life when speaking Biblical, positive words to them. We can see depression and anxiety fade away and unwavering hope enter into their hearts. We experience positive attraction when speaking positive words unto others. My experience has indicated that when I comfort, uplift, and exhort others, I, too, am comforted, uplifted, and exhorted by Jesus because I am obedient in spreading his love.

If you would like more information or would like to schedule a seminar with Pastor Jan Coverstone you may contact him at pastorjanc@live.com.

Made in the USA
Middletown, DE
02 July 2021